CONSUMER BEHAVIOR AND ENVIRONMENTAL QUALITY

CONSUMER BEHAVIOR AND ENVIRONMENTAL QUALITY

Trends and prospects in the ways of life

Proceedings of a symposium organized by the
International Institute for Environment and Society of
the Science Center Berlin.
Berlin, November 1980.

edited by
Liisa Uusitalo

St. Martin's Press   New York

ISBN 0-312-16606-0.

Library of Congress Cataloging in Publication Data

Main entry under title:
Consumer behavior and environmental quality.
   "Proceedings of a symposium organized by the International Institute for Environment and Society
of the Science Center Berlin, Berlin, November 1980."
   Includes bibliographical references.
   Contents: Introduction — The materialistic life style / Åke Daun — Social structure, life-styles, and
man-object relationships / Karl H. Hörning — What kinds of alternative ways of life are possible? /
Philippe d'Iribarne — [etc.]
   1. Consumers — Congresses. 2. Human ecology — Congresses. 3. Life style — Congresses. 4.
Materialism — Congresses. 5. Environmental protection — Congresses. 6. Conservation of natural
resources — Congresses.
I. Uusitalo, Liisa, 1944-   . II. Internationales Institut für Umwelt und Gesellschaft.
HF5415.3.C719   1982   305   82-10686
ISBN 0-312-16606-0

Contents

LIST OF CONTRIBUTORS

Professor Johan Arndt,   The Norwegian School of Economics and Business Administration, Norway

Dr. Lars Bergman,   Stockholm School of Economics, Sweden

Dr. Åke Daun,   University of Stockholm, Department of Ethnology, Sweden

Professor Karl-Otto Hondrich,   Johan Wolfgang Goethe University, Frankfurt am Main, West-Germany

Professor Karl H. Hörning,   Aachen Technical University, Institute of Sociology, West-Germany

Dr. Philippe d'Iribarne,   Centre de Recherche sur le Bien-Etre, Paris, France

Professor Jeja-Pekka Roos,   University of Helsinki, Department of Social Policy, Finland

Professor Burkhard Strümpel,   Free University of Berlin, West-Germany

Dr. Liisa Uusitalo,   Helsinki School of Economics, Finland

PREFACE

Environmental policy research tends to focus on the behaviour of industrial firms and government agencies. The behaviour of consumers, both with respect to the evironmental compatibility of consumption processes and to consumers' interest in environmental quality has yet to gain due attention. For this purpose a research area 'Consumer Behaviour and the Environment' was established in 1977 at the International Institute for Environment and Society of the Science Center Berlin.

A series of studies on specific environmentally relevant consumption behaviours such as household energy consumption, household waste and recreational land use has taught us that, in order to understand how and why consumers affect and are affected by environmental quality, we would have to look at overall patterns of consumption, their cumulative impact and the social and institutional structures conditioning them. Liisa Uusitalo, who joined the programme in 1979, set up a study on the ecological relevance of consumption styles, on the basis of her pioneering work on giving empirical content to the concept.

In view of the novelty of the field of study, and in accordance with a long-standing Science Center tradition, an attempt was made at an early stage of study to involve scholars from a broad social scientific spectrum. The present book brings together contributions to an International Colloqium that was organised to confront diverse theoretical perspectives and to focus them on the issue of structural changes in consumption conducive to environmental improvement.

We would like to thank Alison Donaldson for her assistance in editing the English text. With the sympathetic support of John L. Irwin , editorial director for academic books at Gower, it has been possible to turn this collection into a book. We hope that it will encourage consumer and environmental researchers to continue a dialogue as yet scarcely begun.

Bernward Joerges

International Institute for
Environment and Society,
Science Center Berlin

INTRODUCTION

As the general concern about environmental quality has been increasing, a totally new problem area in consumption and welfare research has emerged: the impact of private consumption on the quality of physical environment, that is, on the quality of those collective commodities necessary for sustaining long-term human survival. The significance of this research as well as the interest in it have increased along with the awareness of the limits of economic growth, especially brought into discussion by energy crises.

However, as it has been pointed out in recent literature (e.g. Hirsch, 1977), not only do scarce resources on the supply side form a problem. Scarcity also prevails in the possibilities to derive satisfaction from consumption. What is in principle possible for every individual consumer separately, cannot be realized if every consumer in his/her individual action tries to reach it. For example, individual satisfaction derived from enjoying the natural beauty of a desert seashore or from the convenience of using one's own car for commuting will turn into an impossibility if thousands of other individuals act in a similar way, thereby frequently causing serious congestion and pollution. The mutual interdependence of consumer decisions will probably also bring about an intensive distributive struggle among consumers concerning new types of scarce positional goods, one of which is environmental quality itself.

The solution of these sorts of problems seems to require that, in the analysis of welfare, individual action and individual satisfaction should be treated separately. In many cases individual satisfaction does not automatically follow from individual choices but can only be reached with the help of mutual collective action. This is due to the fact that free commodities, such as the assimilative capacity of the nature are treated as external to economic decision-making when individuals make their choices. This failure, which seems to be as if "built in" the market mechanism, leads to a misallocation of resources in society (see e.g. Ayres and Kneese 1969). For example, the structure of consumption would be different from what it is presently if all negative external effects of consumption had been taken into account and included in the prices of consumer goods and services.

The purpose of economic growth has long been a central subject of popular debate. Lately, the general growth vs. nongrowth debate has been gradually shifting to a discussion about the possibilities and dimensions of qualitative growth in a post-industrial society. More precisely, the latter involves a reallocation of economic growth in order to minimize the negative external effects mentioned above. Sometimes growth and welfare are seen as contradictory because economic growth tends to intensify environmental damage both in production and consumption. On the other hand, economic growth is usually considered a prerequisite for the willingness and ability to finance new environment-saving standards and practices in society.

One suggested solution to the problem is to appeal directly to individual decision makers as the so-called environmental movement does. This movement has directed strong criticism at dominant life-styles and patterns of material consumption in industrial societies and proposed alternative life-styles. However, current problem-solving and applied research in the field of environmental policy remains, to a large extent, restricted to technological improvement and supply-oriented economic approaches. This depends on the fact that there are rather few studies concerning the environmental effects of dominant life-styles.

In the context of environmental policy, studies of the dominant cultural patterns of behavior, ways of life and consumption patterns, are still rare. Research that has been carried out in this area has often been limited to some specific consumer products or a few isolated household activities. The environmental impacts of some immediately relevant areas of consumption, e.g. private energy consumption, are beginning to attract considerable attention, whereas other environmental impacts of household behavior, both direct ones and indirect ones (e.g. through the reciprocal influence of consumption and production structure) remain largely unexplored.

Economic models have served as a main conceptual framework for studies of environmental quality. Similarly, solutions for the problems of environmental costs of consumption are typically couched in economic terms. However, the implicit analytic assumptions of conventional economic models alone are too restrictive for a broader scale study and understanding of the social roots, consequences and emergent trends of mass-consumption and its impact on men's relations to their environment. The use of economic incentives in environmental policy, which is based on the theory of individual rational choices, does not fully take advantage of other measures than prices which could be used to establish environmentally important norms of behavior.

Other social science explanatory devices than economic models have hitherto only seldom been employed for the particular purposes of environmental research. Obviously several of the institutional and social approaches employed, for example, in present-day consumer, welfare and way-of-life research could fruitfully be brought together to supplement the "mainstream" economic thinking. They would seem to be particularly suitable in analyzing the interdependency of people's choices as well as the social and institutional background of behavior. Conversely, environmental issues, which have so far gained only marginal attention within these research traditions, may well serve as a vehicle of rapprochement between them. The general debate within social science about the features of post-industrial society would thus be enriched by more refined models and theories as well as empirical findings.

Purpose and Content of the Book

This book is based on the proceedings of a research symposium with the same title. The symposium was organized by the International Institute for Environment and Society in Berlin. It was one of the first efforts to bring together social scientists from different disciplines to discuss ideas and formulate problems concerning research in the consumption-environment relationship. Most writers of the book had not been working with environmental problems before, and therefore they were, for the first time, faced with the challenge to link their past or present research with the subject area. The ideas presented in the papers are meant to provide a broad theoretical background for the understanding of the problem field, but there are also papers dealing with empirical results. Due to the interdisciplinary character of the meeting, there is a rather wide heterogeneity in the contents and arguments of the papers. Despite these reservations we hope that the book will give insight in the consumer-environment relationship and encourage further exploration and empirical research within social sciences in this domain.

The book is divided into three parts. The first part consists of papers
critically evaluating existing and alternative ways of life and their
prerequisites. Many authors especially emphasize changes which have taken place
in the relationships between private and public life spheres. **Åke Daun**
analyzes the psychological aim of individuals to achieve "compensatory freedom"
or independence in the area of private consumption, as a counterbalance to or
reaction against the increased control in other aspects of their lives. This
kind of compensating via consumption tends to form a basic obstacle to
environmental protection.

Karl Hörning discusses ideas from a continuing research project in which
the relationship of work and consumption is under study. He presents five
theses concerning the development trends within occupational and
extraoccupational spheres of life which imply changes in man-object
relationships. He also points out shifts in the fragmentation of life spheres
and the consequent shift in control tasks between private and public spheres.

Several assumptions of social and technological background factors influencing
overconsumption will be under critical scrutiny in **Philippe d'Iribarne's**
paper. Satisfaction from consumption will be taken as a psychological state
which is relative to and dependent on social comparison. He also points out the
fact that, in the struggle against overconsumption, varying degrees of
lifestyle changes can be seen as goals for policy, ranging from the more
superficial to the more radical changes in social symbols.

J.-P. Roos first compares different, previously presented lifestyle
typologies and then presents his own typology of the subjective ways of life.
Empirical autobiographical data have been utilized in his study. Four new
interesting criteria were used in differentiating subjective ways of life: an
individual's life control (both external and internal), the nature and number
of life experiences, the demarcation between public and private life attitudes,
and main life (interest) orientation.

The second section of the book contains two papers mainly concentrating on
need differentiation and ongoing changes in need and value orientations of
post-industrial societies. **Karl Otto Hondrich's** paper summarizes
alternative conceptions of need theory. In particular, his paper aims at

describing the mechanism of need differentiation as a consequence of changes in social and institutional structures.

Burkhard Strümpel gives examples of existing types of market failure in meeting requirements of consumers who are oriented towards post-material values. This failure is common for the market for goods, the labor market and the capital market. He also criticizes the inability of political systems to adopt and pursuit new values. According to some explorative empirical results, a gap exists between public expectations and the dominant practices of the technostructure.

The third and final section mainly deals with the economic background of the issue. **Johan Arndt's** paper emphasizes the need for an actual theoretical shift in marketing thought. This shift is needed in order that environmental aspects of consumption can receive attention and become integrated into the evaluation of the performance of a marketing system. The narrow view of the concept of productivity should be replaced by a broader concept which includes the negative externalities of the production and marketing systems.

Lars Bergman's economic analysis is based on international comparisons of input-output macro-level data, and it considers intercountry differences and variations in energy consumption patterns. It seeks to point out which differences are due to basic differences in "technology" and "life style", while first eliminating differences due to structural factors, income levels and relative prices.

Finally, **Liisa Uusitalo** presents some empirical evidence of how certain long-term changes in consumption patterns have increased the negative externalities of private consumption. Examples are provided concerning household waste and households' energy consumption.

REFERENCES:

Ayres, R.U. and Kneese, A.V. (1969) Production, consumption and externalities. **American Economic Review 59**, 282 - 297

Hirsch, F. (1977) **Social limits to growth** London: Routledge and Kegan Paul

THE MATERIALISTIC LIFE-STYLE: SOME SOCIO-PSYCHOLOGICAL ASPECTS

Åke Daun [1]

ABSTRACT

The following hypotheses are presented in this paper: (1) a high level of material consumption functions as a "meaning in life" for many people, i.e. it provides an aim for their daily endeavours; (2) the strong emphasis on private property (cars, single-family homes, second homes) is reinforced by its function as compensation for the experience of restrictions in other areas of life - in working life, in encounters with bureaucracy, etc.; (3) material consumption is a means of holding the family members together and has replaced the earlier productive functions of the household. It is assumed that these three phenomena encourage a materialistic life-style. If we wish to counteract this life-style the following changes would be beneficial: (1) greater cognitive importance being given to non-material goals in day-to-day life; (2) sources of restrictions in working life being reduced; and (3) households regaining some of their former productive functions.

INTRODUCTION

In Western industrial countries there is a dominating pattern geared towards the consumption of material products. A large part of this consumption is determined by fashion and implies rapid changes of products: clothing, furniture and interior decoration, appliances such as radios and TV sets, stereo equipment, cars, etc. Consumers express their interest in buying new products by asking for them. The productive system is also founded and dependent largely upon the high rate of consumption. It is the large volume of production which makes it possible to have relatively low prices for sophisticated household appliances, and which creates jobs for more people than a slower rate of consumption would allow. This large volume also results in good wages and company profits that can be taxed and distributed for social purposes.

---

1   University of Stockholm, Department of Ethnology

It is technological development, in combination with other conditions within the social structure, which has created a life-style oriented towards the consumption of products in both capitalist and socialist countries, but people have simultaneously developed fundamental values which make this material consumption appear unquestionably natural and desirable to the individual. One reason why so few people protest about the poor quality of clothes and many other products is that they expect to buy new ones anyway and actually look forward to acquiring the new fashions.

It was primarily during the 1970s that this system of expansionist economics and consumer culture was seriously questioned and alternative ways of organizing society were proposed (e.g. Schumacher, 1973; Erlich, 1974; Hirsch, 1978; Bossel, 1978; Binswanger, 1979). Among other things this criticism was concerned with energy consumption and its consequences for environmental pollution, as well as with the dependence upon the oil producing nations and the economic and political risks which this dependence implies. Another objection concerns the global imbalance in terms of energy consumption, utilization of raw materials and material consumption generally. Additional criticism deals with the social costs which the growth-oriented economy entails, both in terms of stress for the majority of the population and social rejection for a growing minority.

I shall not dwell on the issue of energy costs for various profiles of consumption here; others have already done that (Lönnroth, Johansson & Steen, 1980). Instead I shall deal with some socio-psychological phenomena which have contributed to the cultural establishment of the materialistic consumer life-style and the consequently increasing use of energy. This process has been especially accelerated by a trend towards **"privatization"** in people's social outlook.

First of all I shall deal with the issue of how a high level of material consumption can give "meaning" to people's lives. After this I shall discuss some special conditions which particularly favour private ownership of cars, single-family homes and second homes. I shall briefly touch upon the basic function of the household as a **consumer unit** and finally deal with some political implications.

MATERIAL CONSUMPTION AND THE EXPERIENCE OF MEANINGFULNESS

A life-style geared solely towards the consumption of goods has been described by some, whether rightly or wrongly, as a cause of anxiety, emptiness and meaninglessness, and thus of the typical symptoms of illness in affluent societies (misuse of alcohol, violence, suicide, etc.) Despite the inability of high individual material consumption to lend a meaning to life, it nevertheless seems to be a way of giving some aim or direction to the everyday lives of many people.

There is a generally accepted postulate that people have a need for goal orientation in their lives, i.e. to connect present actions with the future through intentions, desires, expectations, plans, etc. Thus, present existence does not receive legitimacy and meaning through immediate pleasure alone. On the other hand there is probably some foundation for the statement that the absence of a feeling of meaninglessness is closely related to the marked presence of goals and "deferred satisfactions" in life.

If we examine the historical process of change we find that many of the ambitions which earlier provided direction to people's lives now play a marginal role or have disappeared completely. Several decades ago the lifelong fight for subsistence and survival was the all-encompassing task which gave the daily struggle its meaning. This is still the general state of affairs outside the rich industrial countries. In the Welfare State, on the other hand, hardly anyone has to worry about not having the necessities of life.

Another aim which has lost much of its earlier importance is that provided by religious belief. Earlier, the deferred satisfaction of the after-life of Christian religion and the "investment" in salvation through good deeds gave many people's lives a meaning. Besides, many aspects of human life were considered expressions of God's intentions. Through extensive secularization, especially in Sweden, this kind of experience of meaningfulness has substantially decreased.

A third goal, which has almost entirely disappeared today, is the one which tradition provided in pre-industrial society. Traditions contained rather detailed notions of how the cycle of life should be arranged, its different phases being linked to the family cycle. Working life and social intercourse were regulated by traditional rules too. It might be said that tradition determined careers from the cradle to the grave, which meant that one was socially accepted and looked after if one followed the rules. On the other hand, if one violated the rules, there was a serious risk that one might be rejected and punished with contempt and isolation. There are traditions and norms in today's industrial society as well, but their legitimacy is constantly being challenged by the existence of competing, contradictory ideologies about proper behaviour. The greatly liberalized upbringing of children and inadequate social control in urban society have caused many people to talk of "a lack of norms" when commenting on modern society.

A fourth goal in life which no longer provides any meaning for people in affluent societies consists of collective ambitions of the kind that played an important part during the latter half of the 19th century and the beginning of the 20th. By today's standards the objectives of the labour movement, the trade union movement, the temperance movement and the movements of independent religious denominations were important sources of conviction in many people's lives at that time. Many people viewed the collective goals as their own. Individual action acquired its weight and significance in the wider context which it was assumed to benefit. Collective goals are also often equated with individual goals in times of war or when nations are subject to external threat or struck by natural disaster. A typical example of meaning experienced through collective goals is the popular uprising or revolution. It might be possible through the use of propaganda to induce people to regard political goals as their own, even where there is little foundation for this in the individual's own living conditions. Furthermore, some individuals have political convictions which imply that collective objectives represent personal goals and purposes for them. More individually determined goals in life such as these have always existed.

While all these goals in life have lost most of their importance in the rich nations of the West, changes in private consumption have provided people with a fifth type of "deferred satisfaction". The combination of steady economic growth and technical development established realistic goals - both useful and worthless - of private consumption during the postwar period: larger and more modern housing, private homes, cars, larger cars, more modern furniture, more expensive interior decoration, refrigerators, vacuum cleaners, telephones, electric stoves, washing machines, freezers, holiday homes, TV and colour TV, dishwashers, electric coffee makers, stereos, video cassettes, etc.

Adopting Erich Fromm's attitude, we could add that man - liberated from the necessities implied in the struggle for survival, religion, tradition and community - is now running away from this freedom into the trap of materialism. In this way he can experience the security of accepting the personality offered to him by the pattern of behaviour around him (Fromm, 1941), namely the pattern of material consumption.

CONTROL OVER ONE'S PRIVATE LIVING ENVIRONMENT

Man has always been the prisoner of externally determined conditions of existence. From this philosophical perspective the individual lacks control over his life. But from a socio-psychological point of view, one would be justified in hypothesizing that today, more than ever before in history, the way society is organized gives him the sensation of being subject to events and structures beyond his control. The introduction of the factory system in production has resulted in reduced influence over work assignments. In both this and other fields mass production and systematized routines have strongly reduced the opportunities for individual initiative. Shorter working hours and time-motion studies, i.e. measures which have resulted in a more effective utilization of the labour force, have had the same consequences. The "space for private manoeuvering" during working hours has decreased (Braverman, 1974).

There is a parallel in the public organization of society. The municipality, the state and the bureaucracy of the authorities in general convey the feeling that powerful, anonymous institutions interfere with, regulate and supervise the individual's life. The official power apparatus is growing all over the world, as a consequence of the need for planning of the economy (which is becoming more and more international). But the growth of human and ecological problems has also fattened the official apparatus. Even the creation of new decision-making and consulting institutions intended to strengthen democracy has had the side-effect of generally increasing the power structure "over" the citizens and making it appear boundless.

In addition to this, mobility on the labour market has, in several industrial countries, resulted in foreign immigration. The mixture of ethnic minorities in housing areas, at school and at work is probably experienced by the indigenous population as something imposed on their personal environment from outside. Both the confrontation with foreigners and - to an even greater extent - the presence of social outcasts like alcoholics, drug addicts, criminals and families with social problems in general, seem to be seen by many people as an attack on their personal integrity (Daun, 1979).

Another phenomenon new to modern society is the influence of the mass media - radio, TV and newspapers. People are reached daily by torrents of information about the world. The most long-term effect of this information may be a realization that there are so many "phenomena all around us", and thus the experience of feeling trapped in circumstances which we cannot comprehend, of being subject to uncontrollable events. Many people probably feel very exposed to the threat of national and international crises (depression, inflation, military conflicts, etc.).

These factors contributing to the individual's sense of being controlled - the system of production, social organization, population structure, the flow of mass media - can have specific consequences for private consumption. A privately owned house and the material consumption associated with it provide a counterbalance for one's lack of influence over one's life in other contexts. There the illusion of individual freedom may continue to exist. Housing can be developed as an instrument for precisely such feelings. The individual may feel that, within the home sphere, he can refuse to submit to conditions established by others.

To buy one's own home means that one can to some extent decide who is to be one's neighbour and can have some control over one's physical environment. One can also cater for this need for autonomy by owning a holiday home --rather than renting one during the vacation weeks. "You can come and go as you please," commented one interviewee in a survey which I recently conducted on leisure housing (Daun, 1980). "I know that this lawn is mine, no one can chase me away," another person said.

Privately owned holiday homes satisfy the need for independence, since they can be used at any time; they are available all year round. The individual can adjust flexibly to changes in the weather, unexpected events and altered plans. The person who rents a holiday home is tied in advance to a definite period and cannot improvise. The many possibilities of rebuilding and adding onto holiday homes are also important and in Sweden many people build their own holiday homes.

Private cars, which are linked to private homes, probably also owe their popularity to this desire for independence. With a private car departure times are generally decided by the driver himself. Inside the car he can both smoke and listen to the music of his taste, which is not possible on public transport. It could be said that the rules of conduct and timetables are too similar to "the power structures" and thus cannot compete with private cars for popularity.

I have mentioned the privately owned single-family home, the private holiday or leisure home and the private car as examples of means of satisfying desires for independence and control over one's own life specifically because these means are very energy consuming. They imply greater heating costs than multi-family housing or temporary rental of leisure homes. In addition, low, sprawling housing areas result in longer travelling distances and fewer possibilities for arranging public transport.

However, we should expect to find this search for compensatory freedom anywhere where the situation allows it, even within slightly unexpected areas. To break official rules and regulations becomes in itself a means of maintaining independence, sometimes with fatal consequences, for instance when shooting traffic lights or exceeding the speed limit. Even vandalism probably stems to some extent from the sensation of freedom experienced when violating rules and norms decided by others. To take a day off from work or "play hooky" can also be mentioned as examples, even though there are obviously other explanations, e.g. changes in health insurance regulations or abolition of punishment in schools. The greatly diminished "tax-paying ethic" could also be mentioned, even though a lot of other things, such as increased tax rates, also play a part.

Whether the desire for control over one's own life is a determinant of such phenomena or not, this desire evidently makes a considerable contribution to the "privatization" which is so common to the life-style in Western industrial countries. There are other explanations for this so-called privatization which I have not dealt with here, for instance the urban housing pattern which separates housing from place of work.

THE HOUSEHOLD AS A CONSUMPTION UNIT

With the rise of industrialism an increasing number of households lost their productive function. From then on people participated individually in production, i.e. outside the household. The household was preserved only as a consumption unit and for reproductive and emotional purposes.

In studying the materially oriented life-style, we should bear in mind that the cultivation of interest in the home, its furnishing and equipment, in private cars, etc. has psychological roots in the family's need for common interests which can bring together husband and wife and even parents and children. Leisure homes function to a great extent as symbolic manifestations of the family unit. When the family travels together to its holiday home in its own car, this expresses simulaneously the links between the family members and their own physical distance from the social world around them.

POLITICAL IMPLICATIONS

This emphasis on material consumption is a political problem because it has been integrated into the dominant culture. Thus most members of society consider a high material living standard and a desire for future improvement both natural and legitimate. Most politicians and trade union leaders are of the same opinion, partly because they themselves are participants in the dominant culture and partly because they are dependent on what their voters and members think. Furthermore, the production of consumer goods, single-family homes, cars, etc. is a precondition for employment and a basis for the financing of public services through taxation. In order to effect greater change in consumption patterns it will therefore probably be necessary to change labour market policy and also to find additional ways of satisfying the need for public services (see for instance Robertson, 1978; Illich, 1978; Åkerman, 1979).

Despite the alarming difficulty of these questions, they have emerged in political quarters in the wake of public debate and political reality: increasing energy costs and the future uncertainty of oil deliveries, as well as the global political risks connected with the high energy consumption life-style.

Whether or not the energy question can create the political momentum necessary to steer society in a different direction, it seems important to me that we analyze the socio-psychological setting which encourages the high energy consumption life-style. If it is true, as has been maintained, that the growth of the capitalist welfare economy has been halted finally (unintentionally), what will happen to the many people who have learned to seek life's meaning largely in additional material consumption? Will collective goals be re-established? Can this happen within the ecology movement or will it take the form of neighbourhood cooperatives organizing vegetable cultivation, solar energy production or day care centres? Such trends already exist, but it is probably particularly people who already have a life-style with relatively low energy consumption who are attracted to such movements.

If it is true that the great cultural significance of private life is due largely to the lack of freedom in people's lives (in working life, in encounters with bureaucracy and the perception of the world through the mass media), then we can at least develop a few lines of political action. These will be:

(1) to increase the autonomy of the individual and the possibility of taking initiative at work, and generally to support the individual's direct influence upon local issues, e.g. housing;

(2) to decrease the authorities' control over and regulation of people's activities;

(3) **either** to increase the distances between different segments of the population **or** (rather) to increase cooperation and contacts between them in order to counteract group hostilities;

(4) to decrease the dependence particularly upon TV as a leisure pastime by encouraging increased involvement in neighbourhood and local issues by means of fundamental changes in people's daily situations.

Finally, if it is true that joint consumption of goods (furnishings, leisure homes, cars, etc.) is an important precondition for solidarity among members of the household, then the logical conclusion would seem to be to try to re-introduce certain productive functions into the household.

Households in fact already have some of these functions, in spite of all the deep-frozen food and inexpensive clothing from Hong Kong. The do-it-yourself philosophy has of late become a necessity for an increasing number of people (car and house repairs, installation of wall-to-wall carpeting, cultivation of vegetables, etc.). For others it is a way of affording the kind of consumption that can otherwise only be bought with money.

AN OBJECTION AND A REPLY

If it is lack of autonomy and of opportunities for initiative which nurtures the materialistic life-style, then would this not imply that executives and academics live frugally? If it is dependent upon the absence of influence, why do these persons not have simpler habits? Studies show that this is seldom the case (e.g. Uusitalo, 1979). Well-educated people with high incomes consume more energy than others. They live more spaciously, own more and larger cars, take holidays to more faraway places, etc.

The reply to this objection is that even these groups have internalized the values of materialism. They have learned to enjoy material abundance in addition to power and success in working life. They have not been able to protect themselves from the temptation of even superficial desires, moreover they have hardly ever wished to do so. Otherwise what would the larger incomes be for?

For these groups, however, self-sufficiency, freedom and influence mean that material goals (the thoughts about future purchases) play a subordinate role. Work and not material fulfilment after work, is the most important thing in their lives.

16

REFERENCES

Binswanger, Geissberger, & Ginsburg (Hrsg). (1979). **Wege aus der Wohlstandsfalle** (The way out of the prosperity trap). Frankfurt a.M.: Fischler Alternativ.

Bossel, H. (1978). **Bürgerinitiativen entwerfen die Zukunft** (Citizen initiatives design the future). Frankfurt a.M.: Fischler Alternativ.

Braverman, H. (1974). **Labor and monopoly capital. The degradation of work in the 20th century.** New York: Monthly Review Press.

Daun, Å. (1979). Social and economic problems of Swedish housing environments. **Man-Environment Systems, 9,** 195-199. New York: ASMER.

Daun, Å. (1980). **Boende och livsform** (Housing and life-style). Stockholm: Tidens Förlag/Folksam.

Ehrlich, P.R. & Ehrlich A.H. (1974). **The end of affluence. A blueprint for your future.** New York: Ballantine Books.

Fromm, E. (1941). **Escape from freedom.** New York: Farrar & Rinehart.

Hirsch, F. (1978). **Social limits to growth.** Cambridge, Mass.: Harvard University Press.

Illich, I. (1978). **The right to useful unemployment and its professional enemies.** London: Marion Boyars.

Lönnroth, Johansson, & Steen (1980). **Solar versus nuclear. Choosing energy futures.** Oxford: Pergamon Press.

Robertson, J. (1978). **The sane alternative. Signposts to a self-fulfilling future.** London: James Robertson.

Schumacher, E.F. (1973). **Small is beautiful.** London: Blond & Briggs Ltd.

Uusitalo, L. (1979). Consumption style and way of life.: An empirical identification and explanation of consumption style dimensions. **Acta Oeconomicae Helsingiensis. Series A:27.** The Helsinki School of Economics.

Åkerman, Nordal. (1979). Can Sweden be shrunk? **Development Dialog, 2.** Uppsala: The Dag Hammarskjöld Foundation.

SOCIAL STRUCTURE, LIFE-STYLES AND MAN-OBJECT RELATIONSHIPS

Karl H. Hörning [1]

I

In the course of economic and political development in advanced industrialized
societies people's lives are becoming increasingly segmented - materially,
temporally, spatially and socially. This compartmentalisation into spheres of
life is accompanied by changes in the make-up of the spheres. The transfer of
economic contents from the family unit to a different (spatially and socially
separated) sphere largely eases the burden on the social relationships in the
family resulting from its economic function. But the development of industrial
societies has created new social relationships: "Social life outside the work
situation has not re-emerged; it has been created afresh, in forms which are
themselves the creatures of industrialism..." (Burns 1973, 46).

Through the fragmentation into different spheres of life, varying demands are
made on the individual as regards action and interpretation. In the employment
or occupational sector the individual is subject to a number of material and
normative controls. The personal or private sphere on the other hand appears
more "uncontrolled" and offers more freedom of action.

This scenario is reflected in the sociological debate. On one side there are
occupational, industrial, and organizational sociology, which concentrate
almost exclusively on the consequences for employees of increasing
rationalization and bureaucratization. Opposing this are various forms of a
"sociology of everyday life" (leisure time, sport, consumption and so on).
These deal with "soft" aspects of society which, seen from the outside, are not
strictly organized and institutionalized. Connections between the two
"sociologies" barely ever exist, at times not at all.

Why are the occupational and extra-occupational spheres so difficult to relate?
Is it really because one is "hard" while the other is "soft"? I believe that
the dilemma is much more one of the theoretical weakness of the instruments of
analysis. The dominant hypotheses (compensation, extension, isolation,

1) Aachen Technical University, Institute of Sociology

integration) - correlating work and non-work - are not sociologically clearly
enough specified. Reference to the differentiated social structural conditions
and sociocultural orientation patterns is lacking. The level of individual
perception, experience and action is not adequately connected with social and
cultural levels of social life.

II

Therefore I would like to put forward my considerations with the following five
points:

1. The importance of economic factors in an advanced industrialized society
    represents a major prerequisite for the material and normative importance
    of the extra-occupational sector.

    Members of society try to broaden and extend the range of their potential
    against a background of a relative lack of political function,
    bureaucratized administration, high output demands at work and a varied
    and expanding selection offered by the leisure and consumer goods industry.
    The growing relevance of extra-occupational daily life causes their entire
    life-style to undergo a **re-evaluation.** Thus, new interests arise, and
    their life-style becomes less dominated by their occupation and work.

2. The increasing relevance of the extra-occupational sector is accompanied by
    stronger **normative standardization and regimentation.**

    This can clearly be seen in the increasing legal and institutional
    structuring of the everyday sector and in the limitations of
    infrastructural arrangements. It can be added that, with increasing
    segmentation, there is an increase of differentiation not only in the
    degree of normative definition of living spheres but also in the relevance
    to action which these spheres have. This becomes clear if one roughly
    distinguishes **three types of sphere of life:**
    - occupational sphere
    - private sphere (family, relatives, friends and neighbours)
    - public and political sphere.

3. This structural fragmentation is caused and constantly changed by processes which are distinguished by problems of **control.**

I make the following basic anthropological assumption: "In all living spheres man is oriented towards control of his environment; through control he endeavours to reduce insecurity." The problem of control can be seen in different areas. Means of control can be of a physical, material, normative and symbolical nature. Accordingly one can distinguish technical, economic, political and social kinds of control.

As economic and political sanctions have been increasingly separated from the family sphere during the last few centuries, substantial displacements of control have taken place. Thus, private and public corporations have usurped the function of economic control and built up corresponding organizational structures with a hierarchy of control positions for the coordination of employees. The same is true of the political sector. Some areas of insecurity in life (physical violence, illness, old age, poverty, unemployment, deviance, the future) are reduced by political bureaucracies, police organizations and public welfare and educational institutions taking over a large number of protective and organizational tasks. Other living spheres are released from these controls. Whereas control of future insecurity was previously sought through fertility and strong family cohesion, nowadays this is delegated. This releases parents and later their offspring from control tasks, but on the other hand it leads to large direct and indirect investments in the form of payments and taxes (for education, welfare, insurance and other such costs).

4. A major prerequisite for this fragmentation of living spheres can be seen in the existence of **generalized media** and arrangements of exchange, particularly representing money, markets and institutions. As Simmel observed: "Modern life is a credit economy in a much broader sense than merely the economic one".

An extension of confidence is a major condition for the segmentation into domains of social life. The rationalization process (underlying the division of labour) brings about changes in the bases of confidence. There is a growing generalization of confidence away from the basis of specific experience. This process takes place through the generalization and rationalization of the law, contract conditions, mechanisms of market exchange and the symbolic resolution of conflicts.

Claims of trustworthiness must be symbolised. Thus, expert claims regarding trustworthiness in specific domains are supported by symbolic certificates, which require institutional validation. This leads to a **standardization** of **expectations.** If, however, the confidence of the participants in such systems is diminished, fundamental crises of trust as well as intensive processes of de-differentiation, can arise.

5. The fragmentation of spheres of life brings about values and orientations which are specific to their field. These can be attributed to **inclusion and exclusion processes** in social relationships.

"Closed" relationships limit not only interactions but also the acquisition and use of objects. This leads to a typical reproduction of life experiences. These **inclusion and exclusion processes** are of great importance between and within the private, public and occupational spheres we designated.

Thus, historically, the production sphere and the sphere of individual subjective relevance became mutually exclusive. This apparently left the private consumption and leisure sphere available for "self-fulfilment". Typical and functional for this process is the transfer of qualitative motives and purposes to the private sphere, i.e., their exclusion from the public and corporate rational sphere. The indifference of political and above all corporate life towards personal goals is objectively structured. This is the central cause of the much bewailed apathy of modern man.

According to Simmel, "money", through its endless flexibility and divisibility, facilitates a number of economic dependencies and, on the other hand, encourages a lessening of the personal element in relationships between people, because of its indifferent and generalized character. (Simmel 1958, 314).

Elias (1939) attributes the alteration of human behaviour and experience in the process of civilization not only to the "power of money" but much more to the state monopoly of force. Thus "human actions are pushed behind the front of societal life". The banishing of motives and purposes into a 'private' sphere and away from their economic and political connections requires a division of the emotional 'inner world' from the vision of self in the outer world, i.e. the market. Ever longer and ever more intertwined chains of action impose themselves between needs and their satisfaction.

The monopolization of force has been followed by other **monopolizations:** of capital goods, of security in old age, of fighting disease, of education and training. Here we are not only interested in the consequences of these processes of monopolization for the individual's existence, but we also wish to find out which structural conditions of individual existence are related to the various processes.

At least four consequences of the fragmentation of spheres of life can be distinguished:

a) There has been an increasing separation of **goals** and **orientations** which are specific to their field in the private sector on the one hand and the rationalized instruments of the political and economic spheres on the other; the chains of action have been torn apart.

b) The politicization of life demands an efficient bureaucracy. Bureaucratic control however requires **stability** and leads to a limitation of individual mobility and flexibility. The same is true of the increasing development of internal labour markets in large commercial and service enterprises. There, the exclusion of external labour market competition creates stability and loyalty among the employees.

c) Increasing economic prosperity and socio-political regulation have created possibilities of social interaction which were formerly hindered by economic pressure and preoccupation with the immediate future. This has led to a **diminishing** stratum-specific and occupational differentiation in the private sector.

d) But private spheres are only private as long as no economic or social crisis causes the segmentation to be reversed. Thus mass unemployment, rapid inflation or political instability can break down the reigning norms of privatism.

III

The way in which people use the money and time available to them constitutes a kind of **organization of life,** and is therefore one of the ways in which social structure is manifested concretely in social action. For this reason the category of **life-style** should no longer be seen theoretically and empirically as a dependent variable or an appendix to economic and occupational conditions. Leisure and consumer activities should be seen as partial elements of social behaviour in general. A careful consideration of life-style could enable us to overcome the analytical encapsulation of the orientations and types of action existing in different social spheres. However the term 'life-style' should not be equated with 'culture', 'subculture' or 'status group'. **Life-style** refers to common values and preferences, as expressed in consumer patterns. **Values** are conceptions of that which is desirable and valuable. They are socially shared and socially based orientations which motivate individual action and influence choices of means and goals. If life-style represents a pattern of action, values serve as indicators of life-style. But values do not only express a life-style, they also influence, encourage, legitimize and alter it.

One of the central values of modern society still consists of the expansion of demand and consumption of goods. The central social values of 'achievement' and 'consumption' have guided a social system, which through previously unknown economic growth has succeeded in vastly improving the material wealth of its people. The costs of growth and abundance were largely loaded onto the natural environment, which was aggressively exploited beyond its capacities. In order to subjugate nature to the present degree, it was necessary to "demystify" it. The conclusive demotion of nature to the status of a dead object is an achievement of rationalization and monopolization, which restricted subjectivity to man in his private relationships.

But the destruction of nature goes along with value concepts in the private sector of the 'good life', of 'happiness of the family' and 'improvement of opportunities for the children'. The 'moral world' of family life and its immediate settings confronts the economic and political order. The major life goals of most of the labour force centre on the maintenance of a predictable socio-economic order, in which so-called 'equity' - represented by material or psychic investments in personal life - will not be diluted or threatened. The concept of 'having a stake in the system', then, takes on new forms. Certain forms of personal and social values which were previously crucial for adequate performance in the structures of industrialism are no longer required. A degree of 'cultural deviation' which was earlier 'subversive' now becomes a form of recreational leisure in which large degrees of freedom in consumption and expression are easily tolerated.

IV

What is the relevance of these developments for the questions we are dealing with? The emphasis on the need for a change of values and a search for alternative life-styles is one answer (e.g. Cotgrove and Duff 1980). In my view there are two much more important processes which can be discerned **between** the dissociated spheres. The one process I shall call the "socio-cultural incorporation of objects" and the other the "professionalization of extra-occupational life spheres". Both processes refer to a connection between private goals and rationalized public activities. Both processes centre on the de-differentiation of the sectors, on an **interpenetration** of one sphere of action by certain elements and media of the other.

1. The process of **"socio-cultural incorporation of objects"** may contribute to their de-instrumentalization. Only if objects are freed from their totally instrumentalized status, can they be dealt with less aggressively. The meaning of wealth has already undergone a profound transformation from the viewpoint of the individual. Where affluence is attained it is increasingly difficult for people to acquire and sustain prestige-retainers and to keep them for a while. One of the striking aspects of modern society is that life-styles vary a great deal less between social strata.

The competition for prestige can nevertheless assume novel forms, as can be seen in the tendency in industrial society towards a concentration of power. The market economy creates sufficient income to reduce the value of income; and, in so doing, it may open ways for the pursuit of other values and ideas, which the market has tended to diminish along the way. Theory and analysis must finally recognize this development. **Objects may serve extremely different purposes.** But having accepted the socio-cultural character of material objects, analysis must include goals and norms as well as the social structural setting in which objects are produced and become part of social action.

This becomes particularly apparent when the terms economic and 'cultural' capital are incorrectly applied. In his book "La distinction" (1979) Bourdieu tries to show the complex ways in which life-style and socio-economic position can be related. He illustrates how different life-styles, cultural interests, consumption patterns and the like vary within a differentiated system of social positions. The combined significance of economy, education and family tradition becomes especially clear.

Insofar as the qualification level of large portions of the population in a number of advanced industrialized societies has been raised by an expansion of education over the last two decades, one can assume that parts of these qualifications are not utilized by firms, but are to be seen as increased 'cultural capital' in other living sectors.

2. A second, closely related yet opposite process is the increasing **'professionalization' of extra-occupational sectors of life.** However, the phenomena thus referred to are not entirely new. In general, commercialization, capitalization and mechanization tendencies are created and suffered in nearly all sectors of life. The significance of the 'informal economic sector', in its most extreme form the gradual 'industrialization' of economic activities outside the market and the monetary economy, (which has only been emphasized recently) could lead to a fundamental structural change in the relation of production to consumption. Gershuny (1978) put forward and tried to verify the following thesis for Great Britain: in industrialized countries there is a tendency to produce consumer goods and services by oneself, with the help of domestic capital equipment. The production of these goods tends to become the sole task of the production sector. The new demand created by growing income is not overproportionally satisfied by services, but by goods substituting final services (Gershuny, 1978, 80).

However, the purchase and continual renewal and extension of capital-intensive goods in households lead to a progressive mechanization and growing technical complexity of the domestic environment. Not only do these technical factors permeate the private sector with principles of efficiency, profitability and time-saving, they also demand considerable technical, economic and administrative competence. One needs this in order to buy proper goods, use them accordingly and avoid unnecessary expenditure. Thus one can speak of a 'professionalization' of extra-occupational sectors of life, which primarily originates in the efforts of the individual to increase his real income and avoid losses (Joerges, 1981, 177-182). If this is so, i.e. if extra-occupational life at home increasingly involves 'work', then 'leisure time' which is spatially and temporally clearly separate becomes attractive, in order to escape the economic norms which have penetrated the domestic sector. On the other hand, paid work itself can take on a new significance, especially if it involves social activity within the firm. If consumption is 'work' then it is to be seen as part of the process of coping productively with reality outside the firm, such as the social and economic infrastructure (for example: the problem of the unnecessary concentration of retailers on the fringes of city centre pedestrian malls, and of shopping centres on the outskirts can, for household and family, mean the bunching of purchases, joint use of the car, redistribution of tasks within the family and so on).

Thus we can distinguish various **strategies** relating to the shaping of the extra-occupational sector or the combination of sectors of life in general (for examples see e.g.: Pahl, 1980). Material, temporal and personal resources can be applied to different goals. The way in which extra-occupational leisure time is arranged has various consequences for attitudes and orientations. The relevance of the extra-occupational sector of life will depend on whether the individual interprets this extra-occupational situation as a burdensome obligation or a realization of his wishes. To this can be added the fact that the extent to which technical qualifications, organizational ability and social competence can be applied within the occupational framework will influence which and how many extra-occupational 'work' opportunities the individual exploits and how he combines the sectors of his life.

Such mutual processes of de-differentiation may lead to a decreasing selectivity between the occupational and extra-occupational sectors. If these boundaries recede, life-styles may take on new forms, varying according to the specific life strategies of individuals and social groups.

26

REFERENCES

Bourdieu, Pierre (1979), La distinction. Critique sociale du jugement.
  Paris.

Burns, Tom (1973). Leisure in Industrial Society, in: M.A.Smith et al. (Ed.),
  Leisure and Society in Britain. London.

Cotgrove, Stephen and Andrew Duff (1980). Environmentalism, Middle-Class
  Radicalism and Politics, in: The Sociological Review N.S. 28(1980):
  333-351.

Elias, Norbert (1939). Über den Prozess der Zivilisation, vol. 2, Basel.

Gershuny, Jonathan (1978). After Industrial Society? The Emerging&
  Self-service Economy. London.

Joerges, Bernward. Berufsarbeit, Konsumarbeit, Freizeit. Zur Sozial- und
  Umweltverträglichkeit einiger struktureller Veränderungen in Produktion
  und Konsum, in: Soziale Welt 32 (1981): 168-195.

Pahl, R.E, (1980). Employment, Work and the Domestic Division of Labour, in:
  The International Journal of Urban and Regional Research 4(1980):
  1-20

Simmel, Georg (1958). Philosophie des Geldes, 6th ed. Berlin.

WHAT KINDS OF ALTERNATIVE WAYS OF LIFE ARE POSSIBLE?

Philippe d'Iribarne [1]

Many people deplore the waste of non-renewable resources and the pollution linked with the dominant life-styles in mass-consumption societies. Moreover, these ways of life evidently cannot provide the inhabitants of the affluent countries with a high level of well-being (d'Iribarne, 1973 and 1975). Thus there is cause to hope that certain alternative ways of life, including different patterns of material consumpion could contribute both to a better quality of life and to an improvement in environmental quality. But are very different ways of life actually possible? If we wish to give some answers to this question, we must examine the social roots of the patterns of consumption which are dominant in industrial societies.

SOCIAL ROOTS OF MASS CONSUMPTION SOCIETIES

Is overconsumption the cause of the various unsatisfactory aspects of life which can be found in our societies, or is it a consequence? Is the emphasis on material consumption a result of the poverty of other dimensions of life? Or are both the consequence of a third factor (for instance capitalism)? Or are all these elements interrelated in a more subtle way?

Some people hold that technical progress entailing the development of large production units, fragmentation of work, big cities and the anonymity present in them is at the root of our problems. Others think that capitalism has systematically organized the impoverishment of workers' lives in order to obtain docile manpower and zealous consumers. Thirdly, one can propose that the spiritual decline of the Western world has led to its concentration on material goods. These theses all rely on contradictory "evidence". It seems that nobody has ever in fact systematically examined empirical facts which might bring the real errors and truths in this matter to light. Instead, each

---

1 CEREBE, Centre de Recherche sur le Bien-Être, Paris

thesis tends to pursue its own path, receiving support from one part of the public, yet hardly being challenged by its competitors. This unclear picture prevents us from seeing how our way of life may be improved.

MISDEEDS OF TECHNICAL PROGRESS?

Much critical thinking has been occupied with technical development, variously condemning its direct influence on the development of consumption.

Of course, technical development has been a necessary condition for the development of our ways of life - at least with respect to their more external aspects. It has led to the waste of material resources, which is now inevitable. Yet it is doubtful whether this technical development is responsible alone for the present situation. By no means all countries use technology in the same way, and it still has to be determined why we have used it in the way we have. In fact, most aspects of our way of life have hardly been influenced by technical development. Overconsumption may at first seem to be linked closely to the development of technology. Yet, overconsumption is observed both in the sector of simple products (eg. meat, most clothes) and in the sector of technically more sophisticated products (eg. cars, electrical appliances, etc.). Even with the most "technical" products we use, overconsumption probably has little or nothing to do with technical sophistication. This is particularly true of medicaments. The various additives to the active pharmacodynamic elements, expenses for publicity and marketing, pseudo-research which creates pseudo-"novelties" all have little to do with technical progress and yet they play an important part in overconsumption (Dupuy and Karsenty, 1974).

A FRUIT OF CAPITALISM OR POWER?

In one very wide-spread thesis (or rather a family of very different theses stemming from one and the same spirit), the capitalist system figures centrally in the explanation of overconsumption. Is this thesis compatible with empirical data? In order to examine this question exactly we have to look at each element of the thesis-complex separately, an enterprise that would go beyond the purposes of this paper. Nevertheless, we can make some remarks which cast serious doubts on the validity of the above-mentioned thesis - or at least on its validity as an explanation of the set of problems in question.

Overconsumption is found not only in the Western industrial countries but also in Socialist countries, now that their "standard of living" is rising. Of course, the explanation for this might be that the state capitalism existent in Eastern Europe is hardly any different from liberal capitalism, and is thus subject to the same kind of maldevelopments as in the West. One then has to assume the joint influence of various elements of a power system composed of producers, the state and the big institutions, acting in about the same way in the East as in the West. How good is such an explanation? Various representatives of the school of thought we are examining here consider that consumption is determined by production (following Marx's classical text: "Introduction to the Critique of Political Economy"). They arrive at the conclusion that overconsumption is induced by the production system, which has an interest in it. But they hardly substantiate this point of view with specific arguments.

In less "scientific" analyses advertising has often been seen as a useful method of bringing about overconsumption of goods. But research done on the influence of publicity permits us to reject this hypothesis as well (as do certain proponents of this current) (d'Iribarne, 1975). Advertising can evidently be employed very effectively by various competing producers selling identical or almost identical products (eg. various kinds of petrol or washing powder), but it seems to become less effective when the products differ markedly from each other (different types of cars for instance). Furthermore it seems to have very little influence on people's choice between large categories of products, or on the global volume of consumption. Of course we can think of other ways in which producers promote their products. But the fact that overconsumption is particularly strong in sectors where producers are very dispersed and where it is not at all clear how they can influence consumers at all (as with most food products) leads us to doubt whether the activity of producers does in fact lead to wastage.

If one insists on this thesis, a more indirect activity can be emphasized - i.e. the influence of big institutions (state, school, church, etc.) which themselves serve the production system. Yet the validity of this explanation is also rather doubtful.

First of all, does it not exaggerate the influence of the production system on the other institutions? It is often said that the production system influences educational development in particular. This seems hardly compatible however with historical facts. In fact, educational development seems to have made capital more reticent rather than more enthusiastic. Promoters of education have apparently been motivated by factors bearing little relation to the fight for increased production.

Moreover, the capacity of the large institutions (school, the medical profession, etc.) to influence individuals seems to be considerably overestimated.

An analysis of how these institutions operate is practically non-existent. The thesis often advanced, that these institutions operate in collaboration with a coercive state, is based on the existence of legislation that favours the ascendancy of the production system (compulsory education, sanctioning of illegal medical practice, etc.). But defenders of this view hardly ever try to study the efficiency of this legislation compared with other less obvious mechanisms. Does compulsory education really play such an important part? It is doubtful.

The same is true of legislation relating to illegal medical practice: it has not prevented the widespread practice of abortion. Legislation can hardly be effective if it does not have the active support of the majority of the population (cf. legislation relating to prohibition); and if one cannot assume the population's complicity with these institutions one can hardly explain their influence.

Finally, does the evolution of norms which are supposed to guide the life of docile workers and zealous consumers really have the impact it is said to have? The theory that the capitalists have brought about sexual repression in order to make the wage-earners better workers/consumers is hard to defend on closer examination. In particular, the fact that the most intensive phases of exploitation of workers tend to coincide with quite the reverse of sexual repression (cf. e.g. descriptions by Marx on the norms and customs of English workers at the beginning of the industrialization period, or the descriptions by Emile Zola in **Germinal**) hardly seems compatible with such a theory.

INTERDEPENDENCE IN CONSUMER SATISFACTION AND THE ENDLESS RACE FOR HIGHER AND HIGHER LEVELS OF CONSUMPTION

When economists talk of the influence of consumption upon well-being, they generally have physical mechanisms in mind: food provides calories and proteins as well as an agreeable taste, a house gives shelter against cold and rain, medicine protects man from germs, etc. But the effects of consumption are not all of this kind. Consumption also affects the individual's psychological state [1]. Its influence on social status, which is well known, is not the only one of this kind, and perhaps not even the main one. One key influence stems from the fact that the final consumer is often not identical with the person who buys or prescribes the good consumed, and that the latter person's choice is a sign of his attitude to the former. The food a housewife prepares testifies to her being a "better" or "poorer" wife and mother (d'Iribarne 1977), the medicine a doctor prescribes indicates the degree of concern he shows for his patient (Dupuy and Karsenty, 1974). Moreover, the objects we use affect our psychological state not only in connection with our relations with others and with the effects they may have on others. A high-powered car or a highly automated piece of machinery may give us an added sense of power and make us feel good, even if no-one sees us. It would be a mistake to reduce these "extra-utilitarian" effects of consumption to its mere influence on social status.

The strength of these psychological effects of consumption is further enhanced by the fact that even those effects that one might be tempted to describe as purely physical are themselves influenced by psychological factors. For instance, a meal may prove indigestible and we may not like its taste at all if it is not psychologically gratifying. Medicine influences our health not only by its pharmacodynamic effects, but also by a placebo affect which depends upon psychological factors.

In many cases, especially in industrial societies, the significance attached at any given moment to a particular group of goods is affected by the general average level of consumption. This fact indicates the interdependence between consumer satisfaction and external effects.

Let us take consumption as a sign of social position, e.g. of a person's belonging to the ruling class or to some particular group of the middle classes or to the working class. It is the relative level of an individual's consumption in comparison with the consumption of other members of society which "classifies" him. It helps him to find his place in a group of higher or lower rank and influences the reactions of others in anonymous encounters. The performance X is a function of $q_j / \bar{q}$.[2] These are the external psychological effects which have long been acknowledged and which[3] represent only one member of a large family of relationships.

Similar effects, and performances which are functions of q_j / q, are to be observed when goods are a sign of the attention paid by the buyer to the future user (e.g., in the case of gifts). Of course the spirit in which a thing is given may matter more than the thing itself, and a shabby gift does not demonstrate that much effort has been taken. Now, whether something is regarded as shabby or generous depends on what counts as "normal", that is, normal in the social group to which a person belongs (Durkheim 1895). Again, the effects obtained with certain goods depend upon how these goods stand in relation to those used by others for the same purpose. How the food a woman provides for her family compares with the "normal" food consumption of her social reference group indicates whether she is a caring or a negligent housewife.

There are plenty of other examples. What gives the motorist the feeling of being on top of the world? Is it the power and speed of his car compared with other cars on the road, the knowledge that he can overtake others or must "allow" others to overtake him? Again, performances are functions of $q_j / \bar{q}$. But there is no need for further examples, for the phenomenon in question rests upon a very general mechanism. In all systems of signs, the meaning associated with any given sign depends upon the latter's location in the system's whole set of signs. When certain features of objects signify something, this something depends on their relative position compared with the features of other objects. More especially, where more of a feature is associated with a higher price, this feature signals relative and not absolute performance. Calory intake, the size of a house or apartment and certain refinements of dress signify general success or failure only to the extent that they diverge from the "normal", i.e. the "prevailing average".

Generally speaking, performance is always a function of q_j / $\bar{q}$ whenever the consumption performance of an object owes some of its significance to its relative position on a scale of prices. We shall call such effects of consumption sign effects. Their existence implies total social interdependence of consumer satisfactions. If we want to find out, with reference to all the effects of consumption, whether any given society is closer to the situation of independent ($U_j = f(q_j)$) or socially interdependent satisfactions ($U_j = f(q_j / \bar{q})$), we must ascertain the relative weight of sign effects in U_j, taking account both of their direct and their indirect repercussions (via their bearing on physical effects).

In fact, current research on various categories of goods confirms the importance of sign effects. Many studies suggest that the dominant role they play in relation to physical effects is quite common in our societies. In fields where equivalent or near-equivalent physical effects cannot be obtained at much lower expense (housing, transport), there is considerable physical interdependence due to congestion and overcrowding. In view of all these facts it appears certain, even at this early stage of research, that reality is much closer to perfect interdependence of satisfactions, with utility functions of the kind $U_j = f(q_j / \bar{q})$, than it is to perfect independence (d'Iribarne, 1976).

This fact has a major impact on overconsumption. Each individual tries to raise his relative consumption level and, if everybody does the same, the average consumption level rises without any improvement in well-being. As long as the consumption level goes on rising, it is always possible for the competition of signs to continue. The race stops at the moment when it costs too much for individuals to go further. It is possible to show that, when the functions $U_j(q_j / \bar{q})$ are determined, the equilibrium of the system implies working-hours which are unaffected by the productivity level. At the same time the consumption level rises in direct ratio to the productivity level. Every improvement in this level involves new moves in the consumption race.

WHAT KINDS OF CHANGE ARE POSSIBLE?

It is possible to combat overconsumption with more or less ambitious objectives.

- to reduce the wastage of energy and raw materials;
- to reduce "waste" of time in work and consumption;
- to achieve a better quality of life.

The harder the objectives which one aspires to, the greater the problems one is likely to meet.

It is possible to reduce the wastage of material resources by superficial changes in people's way of life. For example, it would be possible, without a change in G.N.P. or in the amount of time devoted to production and to consumption, to reduce energy-intensive consumption (transport, heating, etc.) and raise consumption of electronic devices, personnel services, etc., which are not energy intensive. This kind of change could probably be implemented by government policy (for example by improving the regulations concerning insulation of houses, or by reducing the fuel-consumption of motor-cars). It is also possible to change the kind of consumption goods which serve as status symbols, for example by a shift from motor-cars to sophisticated electronic devices. A campaign of information about desirable shifts presently occurring in social groups which are opinion-leaders might very well be useful. But such policies or shifts in social symbols cannot reduce time wastage, or improve quality of life. If the time devoted by consumers to producing and consuming energy-intensive goods is reduced, we can expect a step-up in the consumption race, with an increase in the consumption of other kinds of goods.

It is possible to go further: we can reduce not only wastage of material resources, but also of time in overconsumption, by more thorough changes in social symbols (of status, for example). This can involve a shift from economic symbols (especially consumption) to non-economic ones (such as achievement in sport; knowledge of, say, singers, actresses or Italian paintings; sexual attraction; a position of power held in a mainstream or "alternative" organization). In this way it is possible to solve "ecological" problems and "overdevelopment" problems, but not to improve our life profoundly (by diminishing loneliness and alienation).

If we wish to have such a change, we shall meet with very serious problems (d'Iribarne, 1978 and 1980). The realization of our dreams of a better life implies on the one hand more personal freedom and on the other hand more solidarity and human warmth. It is not easy to obtain both of these simultaneously however. In traditional societies social bonds are strong but people have very little personal freedom. In the transition from the "gemeinschaft" ("community") of "traditional" societies to the "gesellschaft" ("society") of "modern" ones, we have found new devices for combatting violence (Tönnies, 1887). These devices permit a combination of a high level of security with a high level of political and social freedom; but we have to pay a high price to obtain this rare combination. People do not place high claims on each other because what happens to others "is not their problem". Freedom and lack of human warmth are very closely linked. At the same time external freedom is linked to the strength of internal self control and to the feeling of alienation connected with this strength; and self control tends to lead to impersonal relationships among people "doing their duty" rather than to very lively and intimate contact.

We would dearly like to go further and build a society where peace is paid for neither by the sacrifice of our freedom, nor by an impoverishment of our life. But is such a change in our life possible? If we dream about it, it is perhaps because the gospel creates an image of a life full of love, containing at the same time peace and human warmth, without moral laws, political power or social pressure. But it seems impossible to move towards such an ideal without radical changes in our deepest attitudes.

The gospel tells us not to take part in the search for domination and power. It teaches that it is impossible to obtain something valuable by commandeering a position allowing one to control or to pressurize other people and it teaches how much more rewarding it is to receive those things destined for oneself alone. What is to become of our deepest aspirations, if we do not progress in such a way? Indeed nobody has ever seen the implementation of such a utopia. But, century after century, our society has apparently taken some steps towards it. And why not go further?

NOTES

1) The mechanism concerned will here be discussed in a very summary way. For a more detailed discussion, see d'Iribarne, 1972 and 1973

2) q_j = individual j's consumption
$\bar{q}^j$ = average consumption of other members in society or reference group

3) In particular by Pigou (The Economics of Welfare) and P.Samuelson (Foundations of Economic Analysis). For detailed analysis, see d'Iribarne, 1969

REFERENCES

Depuy, J.P. and Karsenty, S. (1974). L'invasion pharmaceutique.
    Paris: Le Seuil.

Durkheim, E. (1895). Les règles de la méthode sociologique. Paris. PUF.

d'Iribarne, P. (1969). Consommation, prestige et efficacité économique",
    Revue d'Economie Politique, Décembre 1969.

d'Iribarne, P. (1972). La consommation et le bien-être",
    Revue d'Economie Politique, Janvier 1972

d'Iribarne, P. (1973). La Politique du Bonheur, Le Seuil.

d'Iribarne, P. (1975). Le gaspillage et le désir, Fayard.

d'Iribarne, P. (1976). Interdependencies of satisfactions: a postulate
    contrary to empirical facts. CEREBE report, June 1976.

d'Iribarne, P. (1977). Consommations alimentaires et comportements
    socio-économiques", Consommation, no 2, 1977.

d'Iribarne, P. (1978). Essai sur la société de consommation",
    Futuribles, no 93, janvier-février 1978

d'Iribarne, P. (1980). Quel avenir pour la société de consommation",
    Futuribles, no 39, avril 1980.

Tönnies, F. (1887). Gemeinschaft und Gesellschaft.

ON WAY OF LIFE TYPOLOGIES

J.P. Roos [1]

THE CONCEPT

'Way of life' belongs to the group of concepts in the social sciences which are intuitively understandable but difficult to define in a fruitful way. It is not like Truth, Beauty or Quality, which only a Phaedrus might attempt to define (see Pirsig, 1979); but nor is it a concept like population or consumption, about which there exists some scientific consensus.

In the interviews conducted by the author and his colleagues, the respondents frequently used the concept of way of life as an easily understandable holistic description (for instance for the purpose of comparison: "My way of life is totally different from that of my parents"). It is precisely this simple holistic usage that has been adopted by most authors writing in an academic context. For example, Oscar Lewis (1961, p. xxiv) has defined his culture of poverty as a way of life. The concept has been used for want of a more definite, precise content.

The same can be said of the historical usage of the way of life concept. We have a fairly good intuitive idea of the way of life of the Romans, of people in the Middle Ages, of the 18th century bourgeoisie (for the latter, see e.g. Stone, (1979); for the Middle Ages, Elias (1978), Ladurie (1979)). Why is this so? It is because we think we know what was important to them and what were the regular features of their lives. People could be defined by their way of life, not vice versa. [1)]

Conversely, way of life is not such a commonly used concept today - perhaps because we do not know what the essential features of people's ways of life are today. It is increasingly difficult to define a person's way of life, i.e. to tell what is important and central in his or her life and what is not. This is partly because external, physical conditions are not as important as they used

---

1 University of Helsinki, Department of Social Policy

to be. For the majority of people in the past subsistence, with a much narrower safety margin, was the major purpose of life and could only be forgotten for (relatively) short spells of fun and play. We can now say that for most people living in an industrially developed country securing a basic livelihood is not the number one necessity. Their lives are organized for other purposes which may be in sharp conflict with each other.

There is one other very important reason: the separation of public and private spheres (see especially Sennett (1977)) and the increase of self-control. The growth of the private sphere and the need to protect it by self-control has meant a segmentation of the personality - there exists a public person who keeps up a facade to protect the private individual. Way of life is usually a combination of both spheres and thus becomes rather problematic.

A concise definition of the concept of way of life could be formulated as follows:
The way of life is a subjective, specific combination of the activities of the individual, family or social group (with a relatively similar way of life) within the framework of the subject's life history and living conditions.

In other words, the way of life contains three general dimensions: (1) conditions (historical and present), (2) activity (including interaction) and (3) consciousness. In the last analysis it is broadly defined conditions of life, material as well as social and historical, which create a given way of life. But the way of life as we can observe it is a subjective creation of the individual or group. It is determined by people's orientations towards their life as a whole: i.e. living conditions and activities. (Or, as Marx and Engels have put it: "Sie ist...schon eine bestimmte Art der Tätigkeit dieser Individuen, eine bestimmte Art, ihr Leben zu bessern, eine bestimmte Lebensweise derselben." (MEW, Band 3, p. 21; see also Tolstych, 1979, pp. 14-17)). When studying the way of life it is thus absolutely essential to analyze people's subjective orientations.

This kind of definition is linked with the "phenomenological" approach of Berger et al. (1977, pp. 17-18), which emphasizes the importance of subjectivity for the construction of the social life-world, but it is connected even more closely with the Marxist tradition of way of life research, represented by authors like Cipko (in Roos and Perheentupa, forthcoming),

Gordon and Klopov (1975), Yadov and Sicinski (1980) - who all emphasize the central role of the consciousness in the shaping of a given way of life.

Although superficially the analysis of Norbert Elias (1979) would seem to conflict with my approach, I regard it as one of my main sources of inspiration. Elias defines the way of life in the Middle Ages, starting with table manners: "...die Verhaltensformen beim Essen...sind ein Ausschnitt...aus dem Ganzen der gesellschaftlich gezuchteten Verhaltensformen. ...Diese Verhaltensformen der mittelalterlichen Menschen waren nicht weniger fest mit ihren gesamten Lebensformen, mit dem ganzen Aufbau ihres Daseins verknüpft, als unsere Art des Verhaltens und unser gesellschaftlicher Code mit unserer Lebensweise und dem Aufbau unserer Gesellschaft." (Elias, 1979, pp. 87-88) Elias's idea is to show that details (which by themselves appear simple and minor), such as eating with a fork, were connected with a given consciousness and a given kind of life. In other words, subjective structures determine the overall way of life.

A NEW VALUE ORIENTATION

It is commonplace to speak of the new, post-materialist value orientation, i.e. the emphasis on the quality of life instead of on material values (see Inglehart (1977) who has done impressive empirical analysis of the subject, even if the data are rather suspect). As many authors have pointed out, these (projected) value changes are not quite consistent with people's patterns of activity. For instance, Ester (1980) shows how those who professed to have the most progressive values in this respect were also the "worst" consumers. The same has been shown by Ekelund (1980) and Uusitalo (1979).

In other words people have not changed their way of life accordingly. People may worry about an ecological crisis, but this worry is not their major one. It does not constitute a central aspect of their awareness, reflected in their way of life (except for those activists actually practising an alternative way of life).

People are unable to change their way of life, that is, they do not have control over it; or, alternatively, ecological values are not important to them, or something else is even more important.

In fact, we may question the idea that increasing affluence and quality of life are mutually exclusive. This idea implies a reaction **against** material wealth and a shift **in favour of** quality of life. People are not prepared to give up their existing material standards for the new values, but want the new values to complement their standard of life. However, we can assume that "quality" as such could be sought for by people who have given up the material values **in advance** (i.e. before actually achieving them).

One of the dilemmas of quantitative research on the quality of life (exemplified by Campbell et al. (1976) or Allardt (1975)) is that the data explain so little of the variation, i.e. there is much too little consistent variation. Put in more theoretical terms, in present-day society, a random sample of the active population does not vary enough with respect to the indicators chosen. This thesis has two aspects: the differences in certain underlying variables like income or consumption are not very large and the differences in the dependent variables are even smaller. It is extremely difficult to tell how people's ways of life differ on the basis of the normal variables of sociological analysis.

Zetterberg (1977) has succeeded better in this analysis by using the so-called psychographic technique in which the basic emphasis is on a battery of questions related to the activity and value orientations of the subjects. Uusitalo's (1979) analysis of consumption patterns also shows many interesting differences, but even here the data is non-standard, based on household budgets and time-use information.

Yet we know that ways of life differ considerably. People with similar incomes, houses, basic necessities and so on may have very different ways of life. These differences in their ways of life can only be described by means of qualitative data for the time-being, that is, until we can establish some measurable differences which correlate with the qualitative dimensions.

For instance many authors have pointed out the importance of the possession of a private car as an indicator of a wholly different way of life. But this is valid only in societies where the automobile is not yet universal. (For Finland, see Uusitalo (1979); more generally, see e.g. Lefebvre (1972, pp. 141-143).

LIFE-STYLE TYPOLOGIES

Zetterberg (1977) has distinguished between the following individual life-style orientations:

- work-oriented style
- consumption-oriented style
- food-oriented style
- family-life-oriented style
- socially oriented style (friends, parties etc.)
- participation-oriented style
- sport-oriented style
- nature buffs
- religious style

It is also possible to combine two or more orientations (38 % of the respondents in fact did this).

Zetterberg also analyses the basic characteristics of these life-style groups in much the same way as Uusitalo does. He shows for instance that the work-oriented life-style is most rare in the working class and most common in the upper middle class (14 % compared to 25 %). In the same way 'consumer' orientation is most common in the "upper class", except for so-called critical consumers who are most common in the working class. The difference is even clearer with respect to food orientation which accounted for 14 % of the upper class (the Swedish social group I) and 6 % of the working class.

The notable thing about this typology is its crude empirical nature. The "theory" lies in the linear factor model and in the formulation of the attitude statements. Yet the picture is very familiar. We have the three major pillars of modern society contending for the basic orientation: **work, consumption and family**. According to Zetterberg and most other observers, work as life orientation is rapidly disappearing and consumption is growing. In many cases we can easily see that Zetterberg's data too disprove the thesis that quality of life is incompatible with material values. The people with the highest material position are also in the lead when it comes to actual consumption **orientation**. Perhaps it is exactly these people who speak most strongly in favour of the new orientation towards quality. Zetterberg says little about the family. However, it is to be expected that family/consumption combinations will grow in significance.

The remaining groups - participation, exercise, nature and religion - are those among which the new life-styles have been sought. Yet they are in a clear minority. They could easily be called the "quality styles" in the modern sense. Work orientation is the traditional quality orientation but not the first one which comes to mind when people speak about quality of life nowadays. Yet perhaps it should be.

In any case, on the basis of Zetterberg's work we can identify the main life orientations and their relative importance for our way of life typology.

Bourdieu has in his **magnum opus** (1979, pp. 140-141) presented a grand tableau in which life-styles and social positions are combined in a table of socio-psychological class structure. The main axes of this tableau are economic and cultural capital and volume of capital. The horizontal dimension is a combination of economic and cultural capital: on the left-hand side is the pure intelligentsia with no economic basis, on the right-hand side the pure businessman with no cultural "capital". The vertical axis shows the economic class divisions. Thus, Bourdieu does not create a life-style typology which is distinct from class: he shows the different ways of life against the background of a complicated socio-cultural class system (what Giddens (1973, p. 107) would call class structuration). His idea is to show how cultural interests, consumption styles, tastes etc. differ according to class.

Bourdieu presents a picture of the diversity of life-styles according to socio-economic position, but not a straight typology. Yet his tableau provides important material for the development of a typology, especially the combined importance of economic position and education plus family tradition (and the vast distance between social groups).

Uusitalo's study (1979) contains a relatively complex typology based on three dimensions: "modernity", "variability", and "mobility". The dimensions are based on empirically derived major differences in households' expenditure allocation. I shall take the liberty of reinterpreting her data to obtain a typology more relevant for my purposes.

As to its contents, it is closely related to Bourdieu's tableau but is less culture-specific. Uusitalo does not list items of consumption - instead she refers to consumption and time-use patterns - but still her results resemble Bourdieu's in many ways.

In Uusitalo's typology (1979, pp. 137-140, App. 22, 23) consumption orientation is clearly class-specific. Maximum consumption-orientation is present in the active, fully-fledged consumers with many-sided activities and high consumption levels; their life-styles vary from less urbanized and more family-centred to more urbanized and less family-centred (the categories "materialized", "young conspicuous" and "active family" falling in between); their occupations stretch from entrepreneur, wealthy farmer, manager and higher administrative personnel to clerical and skilled workers ("affluent workers").

A lower degree of consumption orientation is present in the next group, whose pattern of consumption is largely similar to the first group, but is less active and has less resources for its consumption, either because of lower income, intensive saving (for a house), a large number of children or the restrictive effects of having a car. Also, family orientation is more or less typical (the categories "privatized" and "alienated"). Regionally, this group is more evenly distributed than the first, which lives mainly in Southern Finland.

Thirdly, there is the traditional proletarian-agrarian austere pattern, with low consumption, emphasis on subsistence consumption, low levels of activity, higher age structure. These people live in houses with few comforts, own few consumer durables, spend money mainly on food and some alcohol, have either no children or older children.

Variation within the orientations depends on stages in the life-cycle. Thus it is possible to have a "career" from, say, active young consumer living in a rented dwelling to an active, family-oriented consumer owning a small modern house and many consumer durables (i.e. a "successful" career).[2)]

Consumer orientation is obviously connected with a way of life: for many people consumption is a constituent part of their way of life. Moreover, the **reason** for restricted consumption may well be a crucial characteristic of a group's way of life.

45

Andrzej Sicinski has in several papers proposed both objective and subjective typologies. As an example of the former we shall mention the typology in which Polish ways of life are classified into six groups:

- pseudo-elitist intellectual style
- neo-bourgeois style (e.g. the higher party echelons belong to this group)
- rural style
- traditional and modern working class styles
- mass-media style, mainly of young people
- styleless "style", i.e. a life-style lacking in clear contours (see Sicinski, 1980).

This more or less socio-economic life-style categorization is meant to be completed with a "socio-psychological" typology in which subjective orientations are included. In this sense it is parallel to the typology presented in this paper.

The above typologies are very useful but not directly relevant for my conception of the way of life. It is clear that socio-economic position has a close connection with the way of life, as well as the urban/rural dimension, life-style and so on. Still, a classification with emphasis on the subjective aspect is needed in addition. In order to develop such a typology more qualitative data are needed. This paper uses data from autobiographical notes written by some 100 Finns living in a rapidly expanding metropolitan area of Finland (the city of Vantaa, near Helsinki, the capital). I shall use the conclusions reached in the analysis of these data in order to develop the more subjective aspects of the typology (for a description of the data, see Roos & Vilkko, 1980).

It should be emphasized that the types discussed here are quasi-theoretical constructs. I have classified a set of autobiographical notes with the help of this typology, but the theoretical variables are also genuine, i.e. independent of the concrete reality of the cases.

A SUBJECTIVE TYPOLOGY

In the following I shall propose subjective categories for a way of life typology. The typologies discussed above have been either entirely or mainly objective, i.e. shown the connections between way of life and objective categories like class, consumption, main activity etc. Here I shall develop the subjective gradient, i.e. such aspects of way of life which have to do with life orientation and evaluation.

I have chosen four main aspects for the construction and shall discuss them first:

(1) **Life control** which, according to the data, is evidently an extremely relevant aspect. It refers to the question of whether an individual (or family) has been able to control his life, and feels himself or herself to be master of it. (Control is always a subjective feeling.) Life control can be external or internal, i.e. control of life's actual events or a sense of life control.

Regarding external control, a high degree of control implies the absence of negative, uncontrolled events (failures, lost jobs, unwanted divorce, chronic illnesses, alcoholism etc., not to speak of wars and other events totally beyond the individual's control). According to my data external life control has improved historically, so that today's young generation possesses a high degree of control (with many uncertainties). The older and poorer people are, the less control they have had over their lives.

Internal life control, i.e. control over the meaningfulness or purpose of one's life, is more complex. It may be either genuine or superficial. Genuine internal life control enables the individual to absorb his life events without difficulty and bring most events into harmony with each other and with the purpose of his life. Where such control is lacking, life is felt to be outside his control, lacking meaning. In the modern context, this is often compensated by merely superficial control, that is, by use of a facade. An example is a successful, carefully orchestrated person who keeps his feelings hidden (the "I'm all right, how about you" type) and never acts spontaneously. Such a person knows his role, what is expected of him, and presents his actions accordingly.

Theoretically the life control dimension is linked with some classical aspects of social psychology, as well as with Elias' theories of the development of modern man (from external control to internal, spontaneous control). I should like to emphasize that it is very clearly present in the descriptions. Life control is obviously one of the basic aspects of people's lives.

(2) By **the nature of basic life experiences** I mean two things: firstly, whether a person (or family) has had many experiences or only a few, that is, whether life has been very eventful or not; secondly, whether these events have been mainly negative or positive in character. A negative event would be war, or a chronic illness like tuberculosis; a positive event would be success in getting a job, finding a wife, building a house etc. It might be pointed out that here it is relatively easy to use people's own evaluations of their lives.

(3) As a third aspect, I use the **demarcation between public and private** spheres, or the question of facade.

As Richard Sennett (1977) has pointed out, one of the basic features of modern capitalist man is the increasing separation between the public and private spheres of his life, and the growing role of the private sphere both in a negative and a positive sense.

In order to protect the private sphere, people tend to erect facades or simply keep others out of a large sphere of their life. We can also call this "privatization" which is meant more positively than mere isolation.

In the autobiographical data, this dimension is present mainly in the manner of presentation - whether the author writes without any omissions, or whether he leaves the private sphere out totally. This dimension is closely connected with that of superficial internal control.

(4) As a fourth aspect I use the **main life orientation,** but here only for preliminary classification. At this stage, it may suffice to refer back to Zetterberg's aspects: work, consumption and family.

In Table 1 the different alternatives are shown which together lead to a typology of **four subjective way of life types.**

TABLE 1. THE SUBJECTIVE TYPOLOGY

	TRADITIONAL	UNIVERSALLY HAPPY	UNHAPPY MISERABLE	MODERN SECURE EMPTY (NARCISSISTIC?)
LIFE CONTROL	Bad external good internal (genuine) adjustment	Good external & internal control (genuine)	Bad external Bad internal	Good external Bad internal High superficial control
BASIC LIFE EXPERIENCE	Full, eventful life with well-assimilated positive & negative experiences	Full, eventful life with mainly positive experiences	Mainly negative life experiences (or seen as negative)	Uneventful life Success Good front Problems with interaction
DEMARCATION BETWEEN PUBLIC & PRIVATE SPHERES	Little or medium demarcation	Little demarcation	Private sphere almost exclusive No public sphere	Very high demarcation
MAIN LIFE ORIENTATION (FURTHER DISTINCTIONS POSSIBLE DEPENDING ON LIFE STAGE & GENERATION)	Family Work House/home (Education a major disappointment)	Work Family Community (Activity-interaction) Education a successful event	Empty or incoherent (Family as the last life saver) Interaction	Achievements Self-consciousness Facade consumption House or apartment acquisition a successful event

(1) The **traditional type:** low external but genuine internal control, weak or medium demarcation between public and private spheres, an eventful life with both positive and negative events, assimilation of the latter. Main orientation in life is not so clear as in the next type, but approximately similar, perhaps with family and family's security in the foreground. Here there are already some alternatives: a housebuilder orientation, a consumption orientation etc.

(2) The **genuinely, universally happy type:** this type also functions as a quasi-empirical definition of happiness, and among any given population it may be considered a rare occurrence. Thus, happiness means high external and genuine internal life control, a full, eventful life with a few negative occurrences, very little demarcation between the public and private spheres (possibly exclusion of the public sphere in some cases, or integration of everything in the public sphere) and a main life orientation towards meaningful activity and interaction, i.e. autonomous work and good family relationships, with some community interest present as well.

(3) The **miserably unhappy type** has bad external and internal life control, an almost exclusively private sphere orientation with no demarcation, mainly negative experiences, a lack of clear orientation. The degree of tragedy varies from complex cases of misery to cases only slightly different from the "modern empty type", but with life's events being interpreted in a different way.

(4) The **modern, safe, empty type:** with high external and high superficial internal control of life, a relatively uneventful life with either negative or positive, but predominantly positive events. The events are also of a less distinctive character. Very strong demarcation between the public and private spheres even within the family. Life orientations vary from achievement (work, home, facades created by consumption) to self, i.e. narcissistic orientation (as discussed by Lasch, 1979, pp. 80-81).

These types can now be supplemented with objective dimensions. One of them is **time,** or generational and life-cycle dimension, one is **sex** (which is not discussed here, as I treat the typology mainly on the family level) and one of them is the **class** dimension. I shall use the latter here. A generational dimension has been added in my analysis of the autobiographical descriptions, but it would require a discussion of Finnish history and so it has been left out here (see Roos, forthcoming).

The class dimension is also based on Finnish data, and as such it may slightly diverge from the standard distinctions.

The following classes may be distinguished here:

- the rural/semi-urban working class
- the new urban working class
- the middle class (employees)
- the upper class
- the marginal groups ("outcasts")
- the special groups: small entrepreneurs, free professions

I propose the following integration of my subjective types and the class way of life typology:

TABLE 2. CLASS-BASED SUBJECTIVE WAY OF LIFE CATEGORIES

	TRADITIONAL	UNIVERSALLY HAPPY	UNHAPPY MISERABLE	MODERN, SECURE, EMPTY (NARCISSIST)
MARGINAL GROUP	NOT POSSIBLE	X "THE HAPPY TRAMP"	XX OUTCAST	NOT POSSIBLE
OLD WORKING CLASS	XX "FORDIAN WORKER"	X "PROLETARIAN UTOPIA" (ORWELL)	X DIE ZERSTÖRTEN (OTTOMEYER)	
NEW WORKING CLASS	X SMALL CITY COUNTRY BACKGROUND		ALCOHOL-PROBLEM FAMILIES VIOLENCE-PRONE	X SUBURBAN, HIGH-RISE DWELLERS
MIDDLE CLASS		THE HAPPY BOURGEOIS	X "THE FAMILY HELL"	THE MAJOR PRODUCT OF CAPITALIST SOCIALIZATION XX
UPPER CLASS	NOT POSSIBLE	X THE TRUE ELITE ("BOURDIEU'S PROFESSOR")	CHRISTIAN BUDDENBROOK-TYPE	THE NEW RICH, SUCCESS STORIES

Thus, for the three main class-based ways of life there are pairs of corresponding subjective categories, alternative way of life types. (The main category has been marked by two x's.) For the other groups, a typical category is more difficult to find.

To express the table in words: there are evidently class-based subjective orientations which are also connected with the development of society. These orientations, together with the class basis, go a long way to building a definite way of life type in modern society, or rather a framework for the description and discussion of actual, empirical ways of life. My point is that these orientations are the rule - the exceptions are possible and numerous, but not dominant. Nevertheless, they are rather interesting.

One may ask about the implications of this type of assessment for the "silent revolution". In my view, Inglehart's results (1977) point only to the dominance of the "modern and empty" orientation, i.e. that traditional values of work and achievement are diminishing in importance, but little else is taking their place.

Perhaps one could also speculate that readiness to act - a normal reaction to a traditional situation where choices are non-existent - has significantly diminished. We may entertain various pious thoughts about the need to improve our way of life in ecological terms, but there is no real need to do anything. Thus, the connection between our subjectivity and the real situation becomes weaker. (Mass communication has also played a central part in this matter.)

CONCLUSION

Any typology of a way of life is beset with difficulties. We can be reasonably sure that a socio-economic classification will correspond with many differences in people's ways of life (which cannot be demonstrated with the help of normal survey variables). These are subjective by nature, but they can be differentiated with the help of such objective variables as type of work, education, stage in life, place of residence and type of housing. What these variables cannot do is to "describe" the predicament of the people falling into different categories. Here we need qualitative data and analysis. Intensive interviews, autobiographical notes and community action are all ways of finding out the actual differences. The types delineated above are in my view the central types in a capitalist, developed society. The effect of social change, a dramatic transformation in society brought about by changes in people's life situations, can be found by a study of how these types are changing, and especially what is happening to the "modern, empty" type.

One possible line of development is that people who experience the "emptiness" and oppressive security of their lives will try to change their ways of life in such a way that their lives include much more contrast and sudden change. The result may be increased voluntary change of occupation, participation in activities which lead to a change in the whole pattern of life, combination of very different activities, such as farming with a bureaucratic existence in a large corporation etc. The ecological movement has a chance of presenting a viable alternative involving such contrast-management. People take part in the green movement, voluntarily accept worse conditions (make their life less easy and safe) - at least on a part-time basis - and accept collective solutions to further such ends.

The second possible scenario would resemble the traditional model. The present historical situation, in which drastic changes in life situation entailed by external events are rare, is only temporary, and in the future we may well have to adjust to much more serious predicaments than those which confronted people born in the twenties and before. This is the doomsday prophecy, which has subsided a little since its heyday in the seventies, but is now raising its ugly head again. Personally, I hope that this scenario will not come about, but one thing is certain: it would produce much more interesting life histories!

NOTES

1) Emmanuel Le Roy Ladurie (1979, P. 353) asks, "What was it that made a citizen of Montaillou 'tick' in the period 1290 - 1325? What were the fundamental motivations, the centres of interest which, over and above such basic biological drives as food and sex, gave his life meaning?", and answers that it was his **domus** or **ostal**, "at once bulding and family, the unifying principle which linked man and his possessions. It was thus the thing that counted most for the peasants".

2) Ari Ylönen (1977) has constructed a way of life typology according to the residential area in the city: i.e. new working class suburb, a new middle class suburb and the core area. He also presents the "successful" type in a very similar manner.

REFERENCES

Allardt, Erik (1975). Att ha, att älska, att vara. Om välfärd i Norden. Göteborg: Argos förlag.

Berger, Peter L., Berger, Brigitte, & Kellner, Hansfried (1977). The homeless mind. Modernization and consciousness. Harmondsworth: Penguin Books.

Bourdieu, Pierre (1979). La distinction. Critique sociale du jugement. Paris: Les editions de minuit.

Campbell, Angus, Converse, Philip & Rodgers, Willard (1976). The quality of American life. Perceptions, evaluations, and satisfactions. New York: Russell Sage.

Cipko, A.S. (forthcoming). Eräitä sosiolistisen elämäntavan tutkimuksen metodisia aspekteja (On some methodological aspects of studying the way of life).

Ekelund, Thoralf (1980). Possibilities for voluntary reduction of private consumption and change in lifestyles. Nyon: International foundation for development alternatives. IFA Dossier 19 (Sept/Oct)

Elias, Norbert (1978). Über den Prozess der Zivilisation. Soziotechnische und psychogenetische Untersuchungen. Erster Band. Ebner: Suhrkamp Verlag.

Ester, Peter (1980). Attitudes of the Dutch population on alternative life styles and environmental deterioration. Tokyo: The United Nations University. GPID 27/UNUP 138.

Giddens, Anthony (1973). The class structure of the advanced societies. Cambridge: Cambridge University Press.

Gordon, L.A., & Klopov, E.V. (1975). Man after work. Moscow: Progress Publishers.

Inglehart, Ronald (1977). The silent revolution. Changing values and political styles among Western publics. Princeton: Princeton University Press.

Lasch, Christopher (1979). The culture of narcissism. American life in an age of diminishing expectations. New York: Warner Books.

Le Roy Ladurie, Emmanuel (1979). Montaillou. The promised land of error. New York: Vintage Books.

Lefebvre, Henri (1972). Das Alltagsleben in der modernen Welt. Baden-Baden: Suhrkamp Verlag.

Lewis, Oscar (1961). The children of Sanchez. Autobiography of a Mexican family. New York: Vintage.

Marx-Engels Werke (MEW) (1968). Band 3. Berlin.

Pisig, Robert H. (1979). Zen and the art of motorcycle maintenance. London: Corgi Books.

Roos, J.P. (forthcoming). Suomalainen elämä (The Finnish life). (Manuscript)

Roos, J.P., & Vilkko, Anni (1980). Suomalaisten elämä elämäkertakilpailun valossa (Finnish life in the light of an autobiography contest). Sosiaalipolitiikka 1980, 67-95.

Sennett, Richard (1977). The fall of public man. Cambridge: Cambridge University Press.

Sicinski, Andrzej (1980). Dominant and alternative lifestyles in Poland: An outline. Tokyo: United Nations University/GPID.

Stone, Lawrence (1973). The family, sex and marriage in England 1500-1800. Harmondsworth: Penguin Books.

Tolstych, Walentin (1979). Eine neue Lebensweise - utopisch oder real? Berlin: Dietz Verlag.

Uusitalo, Liisa (1979). Consumption style and way of life. An empirical identification and explanation of consumption style dimensions. Helsinki: The School of Economics.

Ylönen, Ari (1977). The way of life and inequality in urban environment. University of Tampere, Department of Sociology. Research Report (no. 29).

Zetterberg, Hans L. (1977). Arbete, livstil och motivation. Svenska arbetsgivareföreningen.

HOW DO NEEDS CHANGE?

Karl Otto Hondrich [1]

This paper will first describe three well-known theories which aim at explaining the emergence and change of needs. I shall then add a fourth one and conclude the discussion with a preliminary attempt at evaluating all four. The paper finally considers whether a change of needs in the form of need differentiation is synonymous with social progress.

COMMONLY ACCEPTED NEED THEORIES

Supply Theory

The first theory I shall call the "Demand-Follows-Supply-Theory". It states that needs arise and change in response to people's perceptions of what they can get. As soon as new possibilities become available, we want to take advantage of them and react by orienting our needs towards them. The theory is based on an image of man as a conditioned learning and adapting mechanism. An extreme version of this is the popular "Manipulation Theory", which assumes that we strive for anything which is offered to us, regardless of whether it is for our good or not - provided it is offered in a persuasive way.

This brings us to the deficiencies of the theory:
- it emphasizes complete variability of needs;
- it emphasizes purely external determination of needs;
- it does not take account of the problem which all persons have of having to choose between different possibilities and established priorities. The theory does not explain why we prefer some available possibilities to others.

Saturation Theory

The priority problem is however taken into account by another theory, the "Saturation Theory" or the "Theory of Diminishing Marginal Utility". This

---

1 Johan Wolfgang Goethe University, Frankfurt am Main

theory, well known to economists, recalls a process familiar to us: if my needs are oriented towards something, then the more I get of this something, be it potato chips or knowledge about needs or love of my wife, the less I am prepared to invest additional costs in it. It provides me with diminishing marginal returns in utility. Increasing supply of a good causes my need orientation towards this good to give way to other new orientations. According to Saturation Theory, we allocate our interest and energy to different objects, that is we shift our priorities and need orientation, according to the level of saturation reached.

At first glance it might appear as if Supply Theory and Saturation Theory contradict one another. The former tells us that need orientations follow the supply of goods. The latter suggests that need orientations turn away from goods as their supply increases. The contradiction is resolved if we look at the kind of goods involved: Supply Theory states that the appearance of **new and different** kinds of goods will attract needs. Saturation Theory on the contrary assumes that an increasing quantity of the **same kind** of goods will discourage the corresponding needs. So the two theories support rather than contradict one another. Supply Theory tells us that our needs will become oriented towards new things. Saturation Theory explains **why** this is so and **when** it will take place: namely when the marginal utility of a new source of satisfaction becomes higher than the marginal utility of an old one.

Saturation Theory has two advantages: it shows us the selective mechanism which makes it possible for us to state priorities within a set of available need orientations. And it suggests that the priorities do not move in one direction: as soon as the marginal utility of a new need satisfaction decreases and reaches the level of marginal utility of another, then this one will get priority again, until its marginal utility decreases ... and so on. So Saturation Theory explains our daily, weekly and monthly shifts from sleeping to eating to making love to working to reading and so on.

One Deficiency of Saturation Theory is that it treats all needs and need orientations in the same way. Like Supply Theory, Saturation Theory suggests variability of needs. However, it does not tell us which needs are more important than others. It also does not tell us in which direction need orientation and consumer behaviour should develop.

Basic Needs Theory

There exists another theory which attempts to do this: "Basic Needs Theory", which is connected with the "Hierarchy Theory" of needs. The most prominent version of this theory is A.H.Maslow's.[1] He distinguishes five needs: physiological needs, safety, love, esteem and self-actualization. They are **basic** in the sense that they are universal to all healthy human beings. They build a hierarchy in the sense that satisfaction of physiological needs is most important of survival and constitutes the phylogenetic and ontogenetic basis for the emergence of security needs and so on. One notices that there is a saturation mechanism involved in the construction of the hierarchy. When all other needs are sufficiently satisfied, the "highest" need, self-actualization, becomes the most important and takes over a steering function with respect to the lower needs.

Despite its many critics, I think the Basic Needs Theory[2] is helpful and stimulating for research. Its deficiencies are the deficiencies of all developmental theories in sociology and psychology: how different needs and corresponding development stages can be distinguished, how analogies can be made between phylogenetic and ontogenetic development, how empirical indicators can be found for basic needs. Nevertheless I think there is overwhelming evidence from child development as well as from the development of the human species that the basic needs approach is essentially right. Children **need** first food, and then security and love, and then the possibility of self-fulfilment in the numerous encounters with their environment. Although they are able to experience all five needs already from the very beginning of their life, growing up means that **relatively** more energy is oriented towards needs for love and self-actualization. The same applies to societies: we can find considerable opportunities for self-actualization in Margaret Mead's Samoan and other tribal societies, and even earlier in mankind's development; but it is undeniable that the chances - opportunities as well as risks - of self-actualization are higher in industrial societies, where a smaller part of human activity is absorbed in satisfying physiological and security needs.

On the other hands the basic needs approach remains helpless in the face of the present-day problems of modern societies, for instance the destruction of the natural environment through activities which satisfy the need for self-actualization. As Maslow states it, this need refers to the human tendency to actualize all capabilities which a person feels he or she has. The desire to be an "ideal mother", as well as the trend towards combining motherhood with a professional role outside the family, can be expressions of the need for self-actualization, as indeed can athletic, educational or artistic efforts [3].

An increasing number of consumption activities in modern societies can only be understood by their direct meaning for self-actualization (skiing, travelling etc.), and others, like driving, making use of household machines, tins, pre-fabricated meals etc., at least indirectly serve the need for self-actualization, by providing individuals with the means and the time for intellectual, emotional and aesthetic processes which they would not have enjoyed otherwise.

So the need for self-actualization, especially when it becomes extended to social strata which were in the old days preoccupied with physiological and security needs, may become threatening to our natural environment. This in turn will stimulate a new need for environmental conservation which cannot easily be interpreted as just another need for self-actualization. The need for conservation is also hard to explain by reference to Supply Theory or to Saturation Theory. I shall use another approach which I shall first describe at some length:

THEORY OF NEED DIFFERENTIATION

The development of species as well as the development of individuals within species can only be understood as a process of differentiation. Why is this? The answer goes back to Charles Darwin. Differentiation gives the living organism advantages: firstly, survival; then, at a later evolutionary stage, attainment of specific goals or forms of survival within changing environments. This argument implies two central ideas: the idea of adaptation of life to its environment and, underlying this, the idea of a basic need for the survival of life. This is the only need which really deserves the description "basic". It can be shown that all other "basic" needs are the result of the differentiation of the need to survive.

Differentiation means that, within a living phenomenon which has all the prerequisites for survival, borderlines are drawn whereby one part fulfils one aspect of the whole survival business, while others do the rest. **Segmentary** differentiation takes place when life differentiates in organisms which are basically similar and independent from each other; it increases the number of organisms of the same kind, so diminishing the risk that life will disappear if some organisms perish. The differences between species increase the chances of survival of life in different and changing environments. The species may thus be said to cooperate (unconsciously) in serving a purpose beyond their own preservation: the survival of life. At the same time the basic and eternal problem of all differentiation arises: the differing parts, i.e. species, may develop goals and interests of their own (first and foremost: their own survival needs), and those particular goals may contradict the survival needs of the whole.

Within species, functional differentiation succeeds by sexual differentiation, which increases the variety of the offspring and gives the species a survival advantage in changing environments. Within the organism of a given species, energy processing and information processing become differentiated, and information processing is in turn divided into genetic and learned information. There are few species, except the human one, who differentiate learned information further into stimulus-response processes and reflexive processes. This step in the differentiation process is evidently a decisive one in the development of life: living organisms are now able not only to satisfy needs, but to reflect on this process and to formulate their own goals, which they express as needs. Only at this level of differentiation do we arrive at the evolutionary invention of what we today call the "person" or "personal system", or more emphatically "personality". It is at this level of differentiation that Maslow is able to distinguish five basic needs - they are the results of the differentiation of **one** diffuse survival need. Similarly at this differentiation stage the chances and the risks of life increase. Human individuals, freed from the instinctive link between their own needs and the survival needs of the human and other species, are able to "self-actualize" at the price of destroying the survival of groups, species and even life itself. This problem figures in topical discussion of an ecological crisis.

At a very early state in the differentiation process - probably with sexual differentiation - the formation of social system starts. This means that living together, or "togetherness", increases the survival chances of individual organisms as well as of species. One consequence of the organization of social systems is a latent conflict between the (survival) needs of the group and individual needs - a conflict which becomes more and more manifest. Another consequence is the way in which social systems have the effect (or "function") of making individual needs conform to the requirements of the group. The differentiation of individual needs has to correspond (within certain limits) to the differentiation of social systems. To put it bluntly, there can be no such thing as an individual need which is entirely the individual's own need; since a newly born human being cannot survive without help from other humans, all needs are from the very beginning formed and penetrated by other humans' needs. What we today call "social needs" in the narrow sense (the need to be together with and help others), can only be distinguished from other needs analytically and, from an ontogenetic point of view, social needs cannot be seen separately from needs of physical homeostasis or security.

At this point a sociological explanation is needed of how needs change. The process of changing needs is nothing other than need differentiation. And need differentiation is a function of the differentiation of social systems, social systems being the most important environment for personal systems. What does differentiation of social systems mean? It means that there is an ongoing, directional process in human evolution. The process starts with small social systems where relationships between people encompass **all** the functions and satisfy all the needs which are prerequisities for the survival of the individual and of the species. It progresses towards relationships or sub-systems which satisfy only **special** needs. Those functionally specialized sub-systems are not autonomous, but dependent on other specialized sub-systems. The family and the clan in much earlier times could assure the survival of their members. They constituted a total social system. When some people began to leave the house during daytime to work together with people from other families, there emerged a different system with a special, a partial meaning: work. We call this process differentiation because the new social structure is different from the old one; and it is this difference which makes " work" appear as a new and meaningful evolutionary phenomenon in human development. Social differentiation permits special and intensified satisfaction within new and differentiated social contexts.

62

There is no basic "need to work". The basic need for survival has led, by process of trial and error, to a social structure which has differentiated activities to secure material well-being from other activities, and proved to be more conducive to survival and more satisfying for the individuals concerned. It is because of this gratifying character of the new, differentiated social structure, that it was able to attract human energy and channel it in a special way which we today characterize as a "need for work". This is a euphemistic way of presenting the social structuring of needs: it emphasizes the advantages of a differentiated social structure over a diffuse one and implies that individuals experience the differentiation of needs as a personal advantage, which they are free to choose.

Historically, this is only partly true. We have to remember that the establishment of working structures was accompanied by physical force and existential necessity, and that the advantages of this process in many cases were and are distributed extremely unequally and, as we see it today, unfairly⁴⁾. The need to work and to enter ever more differentiated working structures is for most people primarily a product of social and natural constraints. However, this necessity can, under certain conditions, be internalized as a pleasure and an intrinsic reward, as Max Weber argued in the context of the Protestant ethic. What has been said about the need to work may be generalized as follows: The social structuring of needs (identical with the change of needs and the emergence of special needs by differentiation of the basic need for survival) is ambivalent. It means a simultaneous increase of satisfaction and constraints for one individual, but also frequently satisfaction for some and constraints for other individuals. So the process of need formation is characterized by a basic ambiguity (ambivalence) which might be called the **satisfaction-constraint ambiguity.** It is accompanied by an increasingly unequal distribution of rewards (which may decrease later on with respect to the same rewards and increase again with respect to new ones).

The satisfaction-constraint ambiguity refers to one, newly differentiated need. In the same process there arises another problem which I shall call the **satisfaction-deprivation ambiguity.** It refers to the relationship between the newly differentiated need and the rest of the needs from which it was separated. New, specialized social structures which emerge from social differentiation are able to satisfy one group of needs better (i.e. more efficiently, more intensely and for more people) than were the old, diffuse structures. But the other needs are usually not catered for. At the very moment that a person leaves his clan to go to work for a boss or an industry abroad, or to go to a political meeting with representatives of another clan, he may feel deprived for the first time of the warmth and the physical support of his primary group. It is from this deprivation that the need to belong arises! Surely one may argue that a need to belong has always existed, is inherent to the human condition of infantile dependence. This need remains part of a diffuse and all-embracing survival need as long as there is no differentiation of social structures which encourages some needs while depriving others.

What happens to the needs which arise from deprivation? There are basically two ways they can be satisfied; firstly, by returning to the old structures which become specialized and imbued with meaning. Secondly, by creating new structures which offer new, specialized satisfactions. (A third way, i.e. de-differentiation by revitalizing the old structures, is not really feasible. It can be argued that what are meant by de-differentiation - "Entdifferenzierung" - by some authors today [5] are further special forms of differentiation by a recombination of parts).

Let me begin by considering the first option. All social differentiation and corresponding need differentiation cause the previous social system, in our example the family, to become poorer. It loses its character as a total system. It cannot satisfy all needs, as it did before, in a diffuse way. Just because it loses part of its satisfying function, for instance the productive function, does not mean though that the family loses its importance and impact on social life. On the contrary, the family actually specializes in satisfying needs, especially emotional ones. It can and must fulfil these affective functions more intensely than ever before. To put it more precisely, the differentiation of work, policies, education, science and so on from family life not only leaves a residue of needs which these instrumental systems cannot satisfy; it even creates residual needs for love, friendship, comradeship and so on. Those needs could not have been conceived of in the old days, in diffuse social structures. They are the result of social differentiation. Empirical evidence for this hypothesis is provided by the growing literature in social history, dealing especially with family and everyday life [6].

In considering the second way of satisfying needs arising from deprivation, I come back to the need for environmental conservation. The need for a healthy environment is certainly part of the need for physiological well-being which is in turn part of the basic need to survive. Destruction of the environment is a consequence of intensified satisfaction of other needs and other aspects of the need for physiological well-being: the industry which provides us with electricity, textiles, tins, cars and mass communication, cigarettes and alcoholic beverages, plastic and pharmaceutical products prospered because it obviously had something to offer which was able to satisfy existing, diffuse needs. (I will consider the argument that this was only reached by manipulation later on). Individuals who buy these products do so because they calculate their individual and immediate benefit to be higher than their costs. Costs as external effects have existed since the very beginning of industrialization and associated consumer activities, but they only became a problem along with mass production and consumption. So the need to reduce these costs or external effects by conservation measures is a consequence of extended need satisfaction. The need for environmental conservation is the orientation of a more general and diffuse need for a healthy environment, which is in turn the orientation of the more general need for physiological well-being. Needs change when a basically diffuse survival need becomes oriented towards ever more specialized satisfactions - which, however, by extension to a mass public (need democratization), create new deprivations and the corresponding specialized need orientations.

According to this interpretation, differentiation does not destroy old needs and replace them with new ones. It also does not advance from "lower" to "higher" needs. Better satisfaction of needs through specialized structures brings deprivations which in turn lead to other need orientations - not necessarily higher ones. The need for efficient and centralized government for instance deprives people of the participation they were accustomed to in small and diffuse political communities. A need for participation results - this is not, however, a higher need in the sense that it relates to something new, as some authors imply by describing participation as a post-industrial value [7]. The participation need today is the (re)orientation of a very old need towards ever more differentiated social structures.

A TENTATIVE COMPARISON OF NEED THEORIES

Let us test the value of differentiated theories of need development by their ability to explain a number of empirical findings. In a survey on "Bürgererwartungen und Kommunalpolitik" (Citizens' expectations and local government policy)[8] we asked the question: "Protection of the environment and job security may at times be difficult to reconcile. Would you be in favour of conservation measures even if they were to endanger jobs?" The results show that middle class people and people with secure jobs would prefer conservation - in contrast with lower class people with no job security. The answers also differed considerably according to where the respondents lived. In a big town such as Frankfurt, 61 % are in favour of conservation; some 20 miles away, in Usingen, where the countryside is still more intact, the percentage falls to 38 %.

Supply Theory would imply that middle class and better-off people adopt the idea of conservation from an increasing supply of conservationist measures - a suggestion which does not make much sense, especially since such measures are a public good benefiting all citizens.

Saturation Theory would assume that middle class people with relatively secure jobs get little utility from additional job security and more from conservation. This accords with the **Basic Needs Theory** as far as diminishing utility of value of job security is concerned. But if the **Basic Needs Theory** is completely correct, then we have to regard the need for conservation as a "higher" need, belonging to the group of self-actualization needs. This can only be endorsed to the extent that conservation satisfies aesthetic needs; in fact, conservation is aimed at more basic physiological needs.

This is the point where **Need Differentiation Theory** comes in. It tells us that satisfaction of needs in increasingly specialized systems leads perforce to the deprivation of a number of unspecified residual needs. Those needs become identified as soon as there are social structures which take care of them. Normally these structures are traditional social systems like families and small communities. So the need for love between children and parents arises when the family has become sufficiently free of other functions to specialize in child-parent-love (and love between men and women). The same does not hold for conservation, this being a public good which small groups do not feel responsible for. As a consequence, a need for conservation could not be identified were it not for special organizations, such as the relevant Government departments and agencies. It is only with the help of organizations that the need for conservation becomes a need in its own right which consists of and recombines elements of needs for physiological well-being, security, self-actualization and so on. From now on, there is a private and public supply of conservation measures, for instance to reduce noise, exhaust fumes, water pollution etc. At this point **Supply Theory** is needed to explain how the needs which were identified in the differentiation process are oriented towards a particular supply of goods and administrative regulations. As a next step, we may look at the way in which different forms of conservation compete with the satisfaction of other needs. **Saturation Theory** or the Theory of Diminishing Utility tells us which needs will be satisfied first: namely the needs which have the highest marginal utility. Which are they? My earlier research on needs was inspired by the Basic Needs Approach, and hoped to identify a long-run priority list of needs with increasing marginal utility. I came to the conclusion that this is not possible. The Basic Needs Approach does not help us, for two reasons: first of all it does not differentiate between needs for self-actualization and does not tell us what happens within this realm or what comes after; secondly, it does not tell us at which point there will be a shift in priority from higher order to lower order needs. So I think the Basic Needs Theory has to be replaced by a combination of three other theories: Differentiation Theory, which tells us how changing needs (better still, need orientations) arise in a continual process of differentiation and recombination of social structures; Supply Theory and Saturation theory, which explain the mechanism of shifting priorities between existing need orientations.

NEED DIFFERENTIATION AND SOCIAL PROCESS

The process of need differentiation starts with diffuse needs and proceeds to specialized satisfactions and deprivations, which in turn are followed by even more specialized satisfactions and so on. Can this process be labelled as progress, suggesting something good, i.e. an advance in human welfare? Or is it at best a zero-sum-game, where every effort for better need satisfaction is accompanied by a corresponding deprivation, the sum of problem-solving and problem-inducing activities remaining the same? The growing literature on the increasing ecological and social costs of growth reveals a trend towards the second hypothesis.[9]

Unfortunately, in dealing with this difficult problem, we often mix up the moral and analytical aspects of needs. It is perfectly right to advance the sceptical hypothesis that need orientations which are formed in the differentiation process are at the least contradictory, and that in the last analysis they go against the most basic need from which they once arose, that is, against the need for survival. It might be argued that the individualization of need orientations together with the hedonistic pursuit of satisfaction here and now make us blind to the collective and future costs or detrimental effects of differentiation. It might also be true that the whole process, with its negative results, is particularly encouraged by organizational and institutional settings like capitalist industry or a "high-intensity market setting".[10] I do not want to argue against those hypotheses here, but it may be pointed out that the negative trends which they emphasize produce counter-effects, and it is indeed difficult to tell where we are heading.

What I do want to argue against is a position which blames social structures (the market, the capitalist enterprise, the ruling class, trade unions, government planning agencies etc.) for implanting **false** needs or orientations in people, needs which are supposed to be "not real" or "not their own" - although they might exist empirically. The distinction between 'empirical' and 'real' needs can be made by two different groups of people: first, by those talking about their own needs. A drug addict may say that his real need is to live healthily like most other people without drugs - in this case I think it is clearer to say that he has two contradictory needs which are both real and empirical: the need for drugs and the need for a healthy life. The difference is only that he **values** (at the time of speaking) the health need more highly. The second group consists of (mostly intellectual) moralists, talking about o t h e r people's needs. Imposing their own moral judgement on others, they call a "real" need what they think is a good need.

To clarify the point further it is not the moralists' **moral** position which
I attack, but their **scientific** position. Theodor Geiger has used the word
ideology[11] to describe an ideological position in the pure sense, that is,
a position which disguises a value statement as a statement about reality. The
scientist-moralist would be perfectly correct to say to the drug addict: "Your
need for drugs will destroy your own health, it is contrary to the needs of
your parents who love you, and it is contrary to the needs of the collectivity;
for those reasons I call it a bad need and will try to change it". He would
also be correct to say that he disapproves of the need for drugs because it
came about by manipulation through a dealer. If, on the other hand, he declares
the need as "not real" or "false", he excludes part of the reality because of
its undesirable consequences and/or causes. This he can do only under the
assumption that he knows what is (un)desirable and that he knows the causes
and consequences of human and social phenomena ex ante - and all this without
revealing to others (and perhaps to himself) all those debatable assumptions
which enter his ex-ante labelling of a need as "real" or "not real"!

Attacking the linguistic and theoretical fallacies of those who take their own
value statements as statements about other people's reality should not divert
our attention from the real problems associated with the juxtaposition of
"real" and empirical needs. I shall name three problems which should be
reformulated for the purposes of analysis.

The **first** one is contained in the question: What are the undesirable
consequences of actual need orientations, for instance the need for atomic
energy, individual transportation, smoking etc. Answering this question means
demonstrating how those special need satisfactions put the satisfaction of
o t h e r need orientations, like security, conservation, physical health
etc., at risk. (Those needs are no more "real" than the needs implied in the
first group of orientations). Many authors are hopeful that the demonstration
of contradictory needs (which they call "autonomous" or "guided reflection" on
needs, or "enlightenment" with respect to needs[12]) will bring some
direction into the differentiation process which might be called progress,
adopting the good need orientations and abandoning the bad ones. I am sceptical
for two reasons. First of all, it is not easy to judge whether a new supply and
corresponding need orientation brings more risks and negative consequences
than advantages. A new medicament or a sectarian community life style might

be very attractive to some people and seem appalling to others - or it might look desirable at first, and later (perhaps too late) be found to have disastrous consequences. Secondly, if the negative consequences of a need orientation are known, many people will still run the risk and prefer this need orientation to a competing "good" one, as in the survey sample where 46 percent of the respondents preferred a tasty meal to a healthy one, and only 26 percent vice versa [13]. This means that additional information seldom helps to bring about a change of needs through awareness of their negative consequences for other needs. Additional information can only be helpful if it presents an alternative need orientation which operates at lower costs but nonetheless satisfies the (less differentiated) background need: a need orientation towards energy-saving measures may be a real alternative to the need orientation towards more electricity or gas heaters - an alternative with respect to the background need for comfortable and warm rooms [14].

The **second** problem for a theory of need change and the question whether change increases human welfare, is the **problem of manipulation.** What kind of measures and techniques bring about a change in need orientations? We shall speak of manipulation if and only if these techniques are intended to form a particular need orientation by bypassing (diverting, deceiving) people's ability to make critical judgements on their own [15]. A need orientation brought about in this way is not supposed to increase social welfare. As soon as the critical judgement of the people concerned is awakened, they will discredit and abandon the adopted need orientation - although in the case of drug addiction abandonment will not always be possible.

How much manipulation is there in need change? We do not have thoroughgoing analyses to answer the question - so I shall only present a few hypotheses: A large amount of manipulation goes on in education - although one hesitates to apply the term manipulation in many cases because the ability of small children to make critical judgements on their own does not yet extend to the future of growing older, and therefore adults may bring in their judgements legitimately. They do not foresee the future in general, but they know what it means to grow older. To the extent that real manipulation exists in education, I assume that it decreases with the development of industrial societies; at least the educational norms strive to give children the chance to use their own critical judgement.

Some need orientations of adults are manipulated, especially by advertising, but these need orientations are not very important, i.e. there exist many alternatives. The more important the need orientations are, i.e. the closer they are to the basic need to survive, the more difficult they are to manipulate. Nevertheless, there is manipulation of very important need orientations, but it only extends to a small part of the population, as in the case of drug addicts. "You can manipulate important needs of a few people and unimportant (highly differentiated) need orientations of all people, but you cannot manipulate important needs of all people". In our daily life as consumers we are all subject to manipulation, but we have an increasing chance of obtaining alternative information and of doing something about it, for instance by consulting a consumer association. If we do not do so, this means that in many cases we value the costs of additional information higher than the risks of manipulation, which is just another way of saying that the manipulated need orientations are not very important to us.

Many consumer and political decisions of great importance, for instance concerning the production of atomic energy, cannot be explained by manipulation (although there have been strong attempts to do so!), but by our existential inability to obtain and to evaluate all important information concerning future developments and by our corresponding willingness to take risks. We know t o d a y that the explosion of individual traffic has brought about considerable problems for our natural environment and we are t o d a y able to do something about it, but I doubt if we could have known this in 1920; I also doubt that an early and widespread, non-manipulated knowledge of the forthcoming problems would have kept the majority of us, as members of the political system and as consumers, from the decision to produce and buy cars. Nor do I see that the societies which are industrial late-comers and which know their future problems (by looking at our present problems) are doing any better. This brings me to the conclusion that the essential problems in need change are not problems of manipulation but problems of economic and political decisions, and that those decisions in a society of mass consumption and mass participation (be it of the capitalist or the socialist type) cannot be made without feedback to the existing need differentiations which have a long and irreversible social history behind them. It seems that those need differentiations develop their own dynamic ("Eigendynamik") which cannot be changed by decisions of a single government or big enterprise or industry;

where is there a society or even part of the world which, in the long run, experiences a need change which is basically different from the change in industrial societies? If it is true that the 'Eigendynamik' of needs is a key phenomenon of social change, then we know very little about this phenomenon.

There is a **third** problem which points to the possibility that need differentiation and satisfaction of the differentiated needs are not identical with increasing social welfare. Claus Offe has recently made the point[16] that many **need orientations are structurally forced** upon us if we want to protect ourselves from the external effects of other activities and general living conditions. As examples he mentions the need for medicaments to protect our health against bad working conditions and air pollution; or the need for a car in urban life. Both are need orientations which he assumes people would like not to have, and which are not their "real" or their "own" needs. I have already criticized the concept of real or own needs. As to the problem of forced need orientations, I think it can systematically be understood within the satisfaction-constraint ambiguity which I developed earlier. The special (and forced) need for medicaments in the example mentioned is the consequence of living in an industrialized context; the decision to live there and to suffer the deprivations involved can only be explained by the individual's calculus that the industrial context all-in-all provides a better relationship of satisfaction deprivation than do all available alternative contexts. Italian and Turkish workers in the North of Europe make this calculus again and again. Where the alternatives become restricted and extremely costly, as is the case for old people living close to industries, individuals still hang on to their poor situation, but the whole group or category of people becomes extremely deprived as compared to other groups. So, on the social or collective level of reasoning, we have again the problem of comparing the satisfactions of privileged groups with the deprivations of the rest. This is the problem of establishing an overall welfare function, Although there is no theoretical solution to the problem, social policy has to make a pragmatic decision to change living conditions for the most deprived groups. A non-reactive social policy may also try to influence social differentiation, by attempting to minimize the negative consequences and the corresponding need orientations, whose satisfaction can only compensate for those problems and does not increase social welfare. Responsible policy makers and their advisors will understand such policy intervention as a very careful process of trial and error; they cannot know all the consequences of (planned) change nor can they prevent all those which they know. Structural constraints and deprivations are, to a certain degree, the unavoidable outcome of social and need change.

Do the constraints and deprivations outweigh the satisfactions? Do new need differentiations indicate additional satisfactions which are, at most, defensive and compensatory satisfactions? Is there no (more) advance in human welfare? My answer is all but conclusive but not lacking personal optimism. Not having an objective measure of progress, I nevertheless see a few possible indicators both of declining welfare in industrialized societies (crime and suicide rates), and of increasing welfare (participation rates of underprivileged groups like women and young people in different roles; longevity; health; security; education). Alternative life styles and need satisfactions have increased considerably and are still increasing - these freedoms have in turn given rise to the problem of stabilizing personal identity by integrating many need differentiations. Subjective indicators show higher personal satisfaction rates in industrialized than in less developed countries, and higher satisfaction for the better-off within industrialized countries (which contradicts a widespread prejudice that economic development does not increase satisfaction). Nevertheless, even if one concedes a positive correlation of need differentiation and social welfare, this correlation may not hold if the costs of need differentiation rise and 'limits of satisfaction' are reached.

73

NOTES

1)   Abraham H. Maslow, Motivation and Personality, New York 1954

2)   With regard to these critics, Katrin Lederer deletes the word "basic" in the needs debate. See Katrin Lederer in cooperation with Johan Galtung and David Antal, Human Needs, Cambridge, Mass. and Königstein 1980, p. 6 f.

3)   Maslow's need for self-actualization seems to be very similar to the need for achievement. See David C. McClelland, The Activity Society, Princeton, New Jersey, 1961

4)   In an historical and comparative perspective this point was made and illustrated by Barrington Moore, Social Origins of Dictatorship and Democracy, 1966

5)   See for example Eugen Buss and Martina Schöps, Die gesellschaftliche Entdifferenzierung (Societal De-differentiation), in: Zeitschrift für Soziologie, Jg. 8, Heft 4, Oct. 1979, s. 315-329

6)   See for example Edward Shorter, The Making of the Modern Family, New York 1975

7)   Especially Ronald Inglehart, The Silent Revolution. Changing Values and Political Styles Among Western Publics, Princeton, New Jersey, 1977

8)   Research Data from the "Arbeitsgruppe Soziale Infrastruktur" at the University of Frankfurt. Some of the results are published in: Klaus Arzberger, Manfred Murk and Jürgen Schumacher, Die Bürger, Königstein 1979, and in: Franz-Xavier Kaufmann, ed. Bürgernahe Sozialpolitik, Frankfurt 1979

9)   D.H. Meadows et al., The Limits to Growth, New York 1972; E.J. Mishan, The Costs of Economic Growth, New York 1967; Fred Hirsch, Social Limits to Growth, London 1977

10)   This is the expression of William Leiss, The Limits of Satisfaction: An Essay on the Structure of Needs and Commodities, Toronto 1976

11)   Theodor Geiger, Ideologie und Wahrheit. Eine Soziologische Kritik des Denkens, Stuttgart-Wien 1953

12)   See the authors in: Klaus M. Meyer-Abich und Dieter Birnbacher, eds., Was braucht der Mensch um glücklich zu sein? Bedürfnisforschung und Konsumkritik, München 1979 and my critical statement, pp. 123-134

13)   Quoted from Frankfurter Rundschau, Nr. 44, 1981, p. 16. (Hanns H. Wenk, Kalorienzählen genugt nicht)

14)   This kind of argument is developed by Klaus M. Meyer-Abich, op.cit., p. 58 ff.

15)   I take this definition from Horst Meixner, Manipuliert die Werbung? in: Klaus M. Meyer-Abich, op.cit., p. 87 f.

16)   Claus Offe, "Ausdifferenzierung" oder "Integration" - Bemerkungen über strategische Alternativen der Verbraucherpolitik: in: Zeitschrift für Verbraucherpolitik, 1981 (forthcoming)

POSTMATERIAL VALUES AND THEIR INSTITUTIONAL INERTIA

Burkhard Strümpel [1]

The symptoms of crisis of the western postindustrial societies of the 1970s and 1980s must be attributed to several causes. In addition to the problems related to the natural environment and the availability of raw materials, there are changing popular styles and goals of life and work, leading in turn to a different mix of peoples' aspirations and demands vis-à-vis the economy.

Characteristic for the decades after World War II was a far-reaching harmony between popular priorities and economic policy. During the reconstruction period, expanding production, based on rapid capital formation, was of high priority to virtually all participants in the social game. In public evaluation the positive concomitants of industrial growth weighed more heavily than the negative ones. In addition to satisfying the basic material needs, the economy provided for full-employment, monetary stability, strengthened the sense of security and continuity. In its first phase, the construction boom replaced ruins left over from wartime destruction, provided dwellings and thus made the formation of families possible. The pollution of air and water, traffic congestion and the noise of the streets remained below the threshold of importance, if not perception. The goal of economic growth reigned supreme. In order to speed up industrial reconstruction through capital formation, German trade unions in the 1950's consistently consented to a massive redistribution of income in favour of capital owners by accepting wage rises far below the productivity increases.

Little is left of the honeymoon of the postwar era. There has been a distinct evolution of values and popular priorities related to the rise in mass affluence of the last decades. These reapproaches by Daniel Bell (1973), Fred Hirsch (1976) and Ronald Inglehart (1977) add up to the diagnosis of a qualitative mismatch between man and the economy. According to Bell the

---

1 Free University of Berlin

successful capitalism undermines its underlying motivation. According to Inglehart, new "postmaterial" value priorities are generated on the basis of mass affluence; they place higher emphasis on those individual and societal causes that are not mediated by material production. Fred Hirsch's concept of "positional goods" is that of the spoilt child: what he has, he does not want, and what he wants, he does not have.

According to the surveys initiated by Ronald Inglehart and conducted in the countries of the European Communities and the United States, postmaterial values (participation, self-actualisation and environmental protection) have been strongly on the rise in all countries, notably among young respondents. Conversely, material values oriented toward achieving and securing command over material resources are more heavily represented among the older generation. Widespread affluence during the period when the younger generation grew up brought to the fore higher-order needs while material deprivation prevailing during the formative years of today's older people left lasting marks on their value structure, in spite of changed material circumstances (Inglehart 1977).

Within less than a decade particularly occupational preferences have changed strongly. While in the middle of the 1960s a qualified majority of Germans and a strong simple majority of Americans had rated economic security as the most important characteristic of a good job, in 1972/3 the item "important work, feeling of accomplishment" had gained ground significantly (Katona and Strümpel 1978). Moreover, the traditional virtues of courtesy and subordination, diligence, modesty, even respect for the employer's private property seem to have lost authority in both countries, particularly among younger people. The number of those who accept "hard work" as desirable and who subordinate pleasure to duty has dimished. The secular trend indicated by Inglehart appears to hold true even when monitoring changes between relatively short time intervals (Yankelovich 1974, Noelle-Neumann 1978). Certainly for many people in West Germany changing values have led to changed preferences directed towards a certain disengagement from the life style of mass consumption and paid work, in short, from a centralized system of production based on division of labour. This trend can be demonstrated both through survey results and statistics, as for instance

- the unusually persistent coexistence of unemployment in desired jobs and job openings in undesired but decently paid and steady occupations;

- the considerable proportion of workers preferring shorter working time under given hourly wages. Asked which of the two avenues for improving the standard of living was preferable: wage increases or reduced working time, the majority of workers in the member countries of the European Communities (51 %) favour shorter work hours over higher wages (42 %); in Germany the respective figures are 55 % and 35 % (Commission of the European Communities 1978). The desire for shorter work hours appears to be particularly strong in countries enjoying a relatively high real income per capita.

- a rate of consumer saving that has shown a strong and continuous increase, particularly on the part of the lower income strata, over the last 25 years (Statistisches Bundesamt).

Indeed, in the real world these changes seem to be largely sealed off from implementation through institutional obstacles. Choices between work/income/consumption and leisure, between income and quality of employment, between material comfort and resource saving counsumer behavior are largely prevented by the well-known roadblocks of oligopolistic interests or sheer administrative inertia. There is a lack of feedback between people and both the market and the polity. What the industrial system has to offer in abundance: cars, refrigerators, air-travel to the crowded Spanish coastline - is no longer attractive, and what would be attractive: an education offering social and economic mobility, vacation in an unspoilt environment, a job that provides decent pay and is somewhat outside the world of large monetarized organisations cannot be delivered (Hirsch 1976). This perspective of reality - to which could be added Ralf Dahrendorf's vision of the work society running out of jobs - leads to staggering demands for institutional adaptation to bring popular demands in line with system output. All these demands are items on the agenda of macropolicies that up-to-now have been virtually monopolized by the well-known instruments of economic policy.

A NEW TYPE OF MARKET FAILURE

However, the present stage of economic thought is far from acknowledging a new demand for free choice. The market mechanism has been praised for centuries for its ability to accommodate the desires and preferences of people in the exercise of exchange relationships. At this juncture the market would have to prove its adaptability by facilitating a gradual retreat from worker and consumer participation in the formal economy in accordance with prevailing preferences rather than making for more production and growth. The inability to move beyond the dominant mode of the industrial and bureaucratized economy is to be demonstrated by turning to the examples of three markets, the market for goods, the market for labour, and the capital market.

The market for goods

Market theory and practice as well as the officially adopted policy of consumer protection are still oriented toward the goal of safeguarding the right of the buyer to choose among the existing suppliers. However, they ignore the task of supplying products or public services that meet the criterion of "use rationality" ("Gebrauchswertrationalität") in the Marxian meaning of the term. They also ignore practices that are called correctly if derogatively "planned obsolescence". It has been carefully documented that the life span of light bulbs, car tires, exhaust pipes, even whole automobiles and many other consumer goods could be at least doubled with little additional costs. The shift towards more durable products would both increase the standard of living and reduce the input of raw materials and energy, and thus diminish environmental damage. The life-span frequently does not belong to those product attributes that weigh heavily in a purchase decision. Thus existing markets for consumer goods fail to activate the technical and economic possibilities for a mode of product development that is in accordance with both private preferences and public goals. In this instance, the private sector deserves hardly less blame for inefficiency than a large part of the highly bureaucratized public sector.

Labour markets

The theory of the market has conventionally tried to create, safeguard and maintain certain options on the labour markets, for instance the chance for the worker to be rewarded according to the "marginal product" of his work. It has failed to pay attention to the existence of such options that allow for a trade-off between work and leisure, or between wage and quality of work. There has been no concern for what has been termed the "time sovereignty" of the individual, i.e. the chance to shape the working time according to one's preference within the constraints inevitably imposed by the production process. In their decisions about labour market participation, people are confronted with an unsatisfactory choice between the extremes of all-or-nothing. Options for part-time work that offer rewards comparable to those of full-time work remain the exception rather than the rule. Vacation rights are stipulated by collective bargaining, sabbaticals are still the privilege of a very limited group of workers, and even the celebrated flexible age of retirement, at least in Europe, is flexible only downward and hardly facilitates a gradual withdrawal from the job. Those overemployed are being prevented by rigid institutional arrangements from reducing their work involvement to a desired level, and others, unemployed or underemployed, mainly younger people and those in danger of an obsolescence of their skills fail to be offered the opportunity to fill in, and thus to serve both their individual needs and those of society as a whole.

Capital markets

It is the rationale of the theory of the market to safeguard options on capital markets; it is left to the investor to gauge the corresponding risks and chances. Yet it is not considered to be a goal of economic policy to maintain competition between capital-intensive technologies that depend for their realisation on massive government subsidies. For instance, if a strategy of large power plants is adopted, then capital becomes extremely illiquid owing to the very long gestation period of the capital commitment. In contrast, alternative decentralized technologies, such as small cogeneration plants, etc., reduce the societal risk of investment failure or, even worse, of becoming locked into an inferior technology for decades. On the macro level we observe government deficit spending to counter the negative employment effect of labour saving investment or, as in Germany, rising rates of saving instead of strategies to create employment without forcing production to rise, such as shorter working time. (Perhaps high rates of saving could be interpreted as revealed preferences for lower economic participation rather than a pathological aberration from a hypothetical path of "potential growth").

ORGANIZED SYMPTOM THERAPY

Those problems that are being ignored by the market are being carried over to the political system. The competition of parties, the classical democratic mechanism for conflict solution has failed to place the issues of growth, environment, technology, civic participation on the agenda of political debate. The available data show consistently that protection of the environment, humane work, participation in decision making, a certain degree of autonomy at the work place are more important concerns for most people than economic and insecure growth.

Although in most countries between 40 and 60 % of the population are against the further extension of nuclear power generation, there is no large party in any industrial country with the single exception of Sweden that speaks out clearly against nuclear energy, no party embracing the cause of environmental protection against vested interests, no party representing the cause of solidarity between the employed and the unemployed, no party advocating the option for a gradual withdrawal from work, for flexible work hours, no party fighting the disastrous consequences of automobilisation or planned obsolescence, of mass marketing and advertising. The gap between the popular perception of these problems and their treatment in the political arena could not be more conspicuous.

The societal alternatives of the 1980s perhaps can best be viewed in analogy to the depression of the 1930s. There was then as there is today a failure of images and instruments that had proven success during the preceding better times. In both cases the crisis has been accompanied by overoptimistic predictions and ineffective therapies, all of them undermining the confidence in the experts and political strategies they represent and recommend. Contemporary leaders like Hoover and Brüning invite comparison with the

Thatchers and Reagans. Around the middle of our century, an activist government sector was able to reconcile interests, perceived earlier as conflicting, and to accommodate popular aspirations, desires and expectations. A new paradigm had converted an apparent zero-sum game into a game with a positive outcome for virtually all players.

The parties representing the main cause of the welfare state have become a major political force at very different points in time. In Germany, democratic socialism became a major political force for the first time early in the twentieth century, in Great Britain only thirty years later. In the United States the Democratic party has adopted late but relatively rapidly characteristics of a party of the welfare state. In all cases the chances for innovation were more favourable than today: well-organised vested interests such as trade-unions and government bureaucracies, together with the impoverished masses rightly perceived themselves as beneficiaries of the new paradigm.

In contrast, there is no common cause of disengagement, of decentralisation, of diversification, of provision of individual options which is capable of collective organisation to the extent required for effective political representation. Judging from the demonstrative verbosity in party-programmes and government bulletins in matters of environmental protection, energy-saving and quality of employment, one may be led to believe that the new concerns are being embraced equally by all parties. Undoubtedly the manifestations of sympathy for the cause of "quality of life" did not remain without tangible effect on the allocation of public funds. Entire industries and bureaucracies created rules and regulations for environmental protection for the treatment of these problems, and endowed budget items for research and development of alternative energies and job improvement.

A routine of attacking the symptoms results in a large-scale "marketing of social problems through the public budget" (Jänicke 1980). According to this philosophy, rising environmental damage justifies the construction of more and larger plants for waste disposal. The problem of mass diseases caused by overeating, overdrinking and inadequate physical exercise is interpreted as a lack of expensive diagnostic or therapeutic machinery or insufficient number

of hospital beds, and the present energy crisis, instead of being viewed as a
problem of excessive energy use, is utilized to strengthen the cause of the
construction of power plants or of exploitation of new energy sources such as
uranium or oil shale.

The vested interests of the organized problem-solvers are intimately linked to
the perpetuation of the problems themselves. The statistics of absenteeism
and hospitalization rise rapidly, almost proportionally to the share of medical
costs out of the gross national product. Also, expenditures for environmental
protection have been rising both absolutely and relatively. Yet the amounts
of most toxic substances emitted into the atmosphere have not diminished.

THE LONG MARCH THROUGH THE INSTITUTIONS

The preceding considerations suggest that the organized problemfighters, such
as for instance the "eco-industrial complex" must not be considered
protagonists of the new paradigm. The partisans of the so called
post-materialists are not to be found in the headquarters of the multinational
companies selling dust filters or chemicals for alleviating the oil pest, or
equipment for the reprocessing of nuclear waste; neither do they populate the
public bureaucracies implementing laws for the protection of the environment.
Wherever they are to be found - in the computer rooms, on the staff or on the
production line, among the "new self-employed" or in the discotheques - they
are unprepared for a battle in the open field of democracy or in the trenches
of the pluralistic, neo-corporatist society. At best they are fit for a war in
the backwoods or, as a fifth column, for subversive activities.

Contemporary political science, to which this diagnosis is indebted, is
devoting large, perhaps excessive attention to institutional interests and
their interaction and has become the "dismal science" of our day. Maybe the
manifest inability of society to preserve its freedom through the recognition
of the necessity of adaptation, can also be explained by referring to the lack
of social learning, of information or communication, of coordination and
cooperation, both horizontally between the different groups or ideological
camps in society and vertically between the public at large and the leadership
(Yankelovich 1980).

It appears that the elites react ideologically instead of pragmatically to the great problems of the 70s and 80s. We have identified three different images of economic and social policy that seem to confront each other irreconcilably with little indication of compromise; (1) the **industrial** vision of the proponents of economic growth, (2) the **egalitarian** vision of the welfare state, and finally (3) the **post-materialistic** vision of quality of life.

These images are supported by certain cognitions which frequently serve to justify self-interest. More often than not, however, false cognitions provoke wrong decisions even measured against the decision-maker's individual or organisational goals. For instance, the proponents of the industrial vision deplore a weakened work discipline for which they blame the extension of welfare legislation. They also hold that a reduction in working time must endanger economic growth and productivity as the labour markets would not supply sufficient numbers of "desirable workers" conforming to the requirements of the jobs. In opposing a shorter and more flexible working time, they fail to consider that the adjustment of time requirements to the preference of potential job applicants helps to "loosen" the labour market, i.e. increase the chances of recruitment of suitable workers.

The public's reaction differs from the leadership's. The man in the street is confused, disoriented, pessimistic, close to resignation, but willing to compromise and renounce ideology. If the leadership has been unable to arrive at a consensus, however rudimentary, about what is going on in society, it is no wonder that the public as well remains incapable of integrating the contemporary economic turbulence into a familiar frame of reference.

This point can be illustrated through some examples of the results of our [1] Berlin exploratory interview.

- Growth means progress, higher standard of living (white collar worker in retail trade, 38 years)

- The economy is no longer a question of real needs. Even with less economic growth, less than the normal rate between 3 % and 5 %, we shall not die of starvation (social worker, 60 years)

- Just look at the unsold inventories of companies like Volkswagen and Siemens. Nobody will ever be able to buy all the cars and appliances stored there. As far as I am concerned, the market is oversaturated. I am an average citizen and have my television, my car, my washing machine, and I only need a new car every five years. Considering the breathtaking speed with which a car rolls off the assembly line - almost as fast as a loaf of bread - there can only be stagnation (concessionary of a cafeteria, 36 years)

- Some say one should pump-prime the economy and create new jobs. Yet pump-priming, pump-priming-where does it end? We possess everything in abundance (ditto)

- I believe before we are stuck deep in the morass, nobody is willing to say: Well, let's make a new beginning (female low-level white-collar worker, 28 years)

- Madness, sheer madness, nobody knows where to go with all this growth (female accountant, 25 years)

The proponents of economic growth of the traditional type were in the minority of our pilot sample of Berlin inhabitants. Their arguments are that growth and a higher standard of living mean progress, that growth facilitates structural changes and prevents unemployment, secures old age pensions and avoids distributional conflict.

Yet the majority of the respondents fail to express favourable associations with economic growth both as an end and as a means of economic policy. The basis of this judgment is the perceived saturation of the average citizen, combined with social and economic consequences of further growth that are valued negatively. The social and economic effects seem to weigh even more heavily than the ecological consequences that are occasionally mentioned. Saturation with consumer goods is not perceived as a purely economic problem. More often than not, a further increase in egotism and loneliness, of stress and overactivity is attributed to further increases in the level of consumption. According to this view, there is a kind of involuntary alliance between those citizens who entertain traditional notions, who welcome zero growth as a kind of punishment for the overextension of demands, and the "postmaterialists", who expect more solidarity and human warmth from less growth. Some respondents appear to grasp eagerly the spirit of the German reconstruction period after World War II. They indicate that the lack of growth would have a purifying effect, in the long run strengthen productivity and re-establish harmony between the economy and people.

Overwhelmingly our respondents feel that any crisis symptoms resulting from low economic growth will be limited. "We will not die of starvation." Rather, there is an association between further unchecked growth and economic chaos. We find combined both continuing positive motivations for individual performance and a distinct scepticism against the aggregate result of individual efforts on the macro-level; the desire for good individual work performance and a negative valuation of the tangible results of these efforts as manifest in the overabundance of goods and services produced. Adam Smith's benevolent "invisible hand" (egotistical individual motivations add up to a collective advantage) seems to be converted into a diabolical "invisible cloven-hoof". This may be illustrated with the words of the concessionary. He expresses himself positively with respect to the individual motivation:

  - "we are still ambitious, I think, and strive and strive..."

However, regarding the macroeconomic situation, his evaluation changes:

  - "at present we've come to the end of the road. This cannot go on. Because we have simply worked too hard. There is no longer demand for all those things."

Some of the respondents view growth and overproduction as a cause of unemployment rather than as a recipe against it. Others, although not denying the threats connected with low growth, unemployment, distribution conflict, loss of international competitiveness, nevertheless do not justify further growth. This is because rather than ultimate disaster, it is just "a little crisis" that is expected to result from less abundance. Furthermore, the threat is being seen as a chance for more communication and solidarity. There is the hope that unemployment can be reduced through shorter working time instead of growth.

In an atmosphere of disorientation, acts of solidarity with others or with society as a whole are not asked for and must appear pointless. For instance, modest wage settlements, according to the egalitarian paradigm, result in an undeserved windfall to the capital owners and by the proponents of the industrial paradigm energy saving is being ridiculed as a romantic deviation from the behaviour wisely governed by consideration of self-interest and thus by the market.

If there is a chance for the paradigm of quality of life to gain ground, it lies in the entry into the institutions of younger experts and administrators who have been inculcated with the "postmaterial" values of environmental protection and disengagement from the philosophy of size. Once these people have become leading experts in the organisations, what Galbraith has called the "technostructure", organisations may no longer be the same.

However, our educational system provides for some people training and socialization in liberal arts, political and social science, psychology or education, to others it transmits purely technical or instrumental expertise in the natural sciences, engineering, economics and law. The first type of education favours discourse, compromise and participation. In contrast, in the cognitive map of technical and legal rationality social conflict is the outgrowth of undue passion, error or ignorance. As soon as possible it ought to be resolved through expert decisions and not through the slow and incalculable working of political debates.

There remain two perspectives for institutional change. First, the professional socialization of the first type still appears to gain ground. The educational revolution of the 1960s and 1970s, the student protest and the "green" movements of America and Europe may become fully effective only in the course of intergenerational change, while the younger are gradually reaching positions of influence, climbing the ladder of bureaucratic hierarchies. It remains unclear if a departure from the prevailing technocratic and production-oriented values would lead into the orbit of the egalitarian paradigma, or if rather the post-industrial value of quality of life will absorb the bulk of converts. Second, in the long run the insistence on the industrial or egalitarian paradigm can hardly benefit those whose interests, aspirations and needs are in the short run identified with the ageing industrial system.

Delaying the advent of the welfare state in the past has by no means been rewarded by a better position in the pecking order of international economic performance. Similarly those attempts are bound to fail that try to solve the problem of stagflation and public sectors. After the world-wide depression of the 1930s capitalistic and socialistic prescriptions paralyzed each other. Only a slow process of social learning was able to bring out mutually acceptable, even profitable conditions. Similarly, the emergence of options for alternative modes of life and work could possibly prove to be the aphrodisiac of the ageing capitalism of our day.

NOTES

1)   The quotations are based on pilot interviews with German respondents conducted in the course of the ongoing project "Arbeitsmarktpolitik und Öffentlichkeit", directed by Elisabeth Noelle-Neumann, Burkhard Strümpel and Michael von Klipstein and financed by the Volkswagenwerk foundation. For the compilation and stimulation in the interpretation of this material, I am indebted to Michael von Klipstein.

REFERENCES

Hirsch, Fred: **Social Limits to Growth,** London 1976

Inglehart, R.: **The Silent Revolution,** Princeton, 1977

Jänicke, M.: **Wie das Industriesystem von seinen Misständen profitiert,** Köln 1980

Katona, G. and Strümpel, B.: **A New Economic Era,** New York 1978

Noelle-Neumann, E.: **Werden wir alle Proletarier?** Zürich 1978

Yankelovich, D.: **The New Morality - a Profile of American Youth in the 1970's,** New York 1974

Yankelovich, D.: Economic Policy and the Question of Political Will, unpublished manuscript 1980

TOWARDS ECOLOGICALLY RELEVANT CONCEPTS OF MARKETING AND PRODUCTIVITY

Johan Arndt[1]

ABSTRACT

Changes in economic and ecological environments demand changes in marketing orientations. In turn, these orientations should be reflected in performance standard or measures of productivity. The present situation in the highly industrialised societies calls for "global productivity concept", that is, one which includes the ecological and social externalities of the production and marketing systems.

INTRODUCTION

The purpose of this article is to outline the potential contribution of a contingency approach to productivity measurement. Our main hypothesis is that there are no such things as a universally appropriate marketing orientation or marketing systems design. Instead, marketing institutions and marketing practices should be tailored to the ecological, economic and social characteristics of the societies they serve.

PRODUCTIVITY ANALYSIS AND MARKETING

It would be most erroneous to claim that productivity issues have been ignored in marketing. In fact, there has virtually **always** been research interest in productivity, from the early writers at the turn of the century (Bartels, 1962), through the monumental "Does Distribution Cost Too Much?" analysis (Stewart, Dewhurst, and Field, 1939) and the sophisticated analyses by Barger (1955) and Cox and his associates (1965), to the contribution of modern institutionalists like Bucklin (1972, 1978a, 1978b).

---

1   Norwegian School of Economics and Business Administration, Bergen

It seems fair to conclude, however, that during the last two decades productivity analysis in marketing has been much overshadowed by fast-growth areas such as buyer behaviour, mathematical modelling, public policy and promotion.

Recently, there have been signs of a revival of research interest in productivity issues, provoked mainly by the apparent stagnation of productivity in the Western world. Though the evidence is mixed at the macro level, there are strong indications of sagging productivity, particularly in the distributive trades (Bucklin, 1978a). The fall often appears more dramatic at the micro level. For instance, today's British Leyland employee reportedly produces only half the number of Mini cars he used to in 1956, despite improved technology and automation (**Newsweek**, September 24, 1979, pp.11-12).

Theorists blame the lagging output per unit of input on major social and economic changes - the reduced drive for efficiency in the modern welfare state, the demise of the work ethic, the corrupting power of trade unions, the shift of workers from manufacturing to service industries, stifling government regulation and unfair competition from low-wage countries. This article concludes that the apparent stagnation of productivity is in part an artefact of a measurement procedure which excludes important costs and benefits.

The contributions of the productivity tradition currently emerging in marketing may be classified into two main groups.

The first category, which may be referred to as the productivity-**in**-marketing group, has mainly been concerned with relationships between costs (input) and benefits (output) within marketing activities. Examples include Sevin (1965) and Bucklin (1978a, 1978b).

A second, more macro-oriented group has focused on marketing-**and**-productivity issues. As aptly formulated by Hilger (1978), the so-called "formative school" stresses the active role of marketing in stimulating economic growth. The "adaptive school", on the other hand, attributes the development of marketing systems and increased productivity in market structures to changes in the economic and social context in which they exist.

This article borrows from both the productivity-in-marketing and marketing-and-productivity tradition. The latter focuses on macro-marketing issues and the interdependence of business and its environment. The former draws attention to conceptual and measurement issues in productivity research. Hence, this article takes a macro conceptual-methodological approach to productivity, without restricting itself to marketing activities.

The point of departure is the traditional concept of productivity.

THE TRADITIONAL PRODUCTIVITY CONCEPT

Generically productivity belongs to the class of performance standards for economic activity, along with market share, profitability, return on investment, etc. Hence, productivity measures may be used in time-series analyses to estimate gains in effectiveness over time, or in cross-sectional analyses to compare the effectiveness of different firms, industries, regions or countries.

More specifically, productivity refers to a ratio between a quantity (total or marginal) of productive input (I) and a corresponding level (aggregate or marginal) of output (O):

$$\frac{0}{I} \text{ or } \frac{\partial 0}{\partial I} ,$$

see Mark (1971), Bucklin and Preston (1973) and Bucklin (1978a, 1978b).

Behind this deceptively simple formula, there is a large number of complex conceptual and measurement problems. These relate to output, input and to the causal linkage between output and input.

Output

In Bucklin's convincing formulation (1978a, p. 20), the real output of economic activity is essentially a service provided - a bundle of items of value to the customer/user. This subjective value has apparently not yet been measured explicitly in productivity research. Instead, different indicators of surrogate measures believed to reflect the value created are used as numerator in the productivity ratio. The set of indicators routinely used includes physical quantities such as production or shipments. For multi-product firms, or service industries producing intangible products, the output is usually a pecuniary measure such as sales in dollars. Obviously, such pecuniary measures should be adjusted by price indices in order to reflect real changes, just as physical ouput should be adjusted for quality changes (Bucklin, 1978a).

Input

The denominator of the ratio is the input (the sacrifices of resource costs) needed to produce the output. Conventionally, input has been viewed in terms of the deployment of "internal" factors such as labour, capital, energy and materials (Bucklin, 1978a). As will be pointed out below, the global concept of productivity implies that important negative externalities of production should likewise be treated as inputs (or, if positive, as outputs).

As usually conceived, productivity is a single-factor phenomenon, evaluating the efficiency of one factor only - usually labour input as measured by number of employees, man-hours or payroll costs. The wider total-factor productivity concept aims at measuring the efficiency of all employed inputs. This broader concept involves important measurement problems, for instance how to determine suitable weighting (Bucklin, 1978a).

Causal Connection between Input and Output

The cross-sectional and time-series analyses (of non-experimental data) normally used in empirical productivity research raise problems as to the direction of causality and the net impact of input factors on output. However, the internal validity of productivity research does not concern us here.

The remainder of this article will describe how marketing orientations have evolved, starting from narrow production orientation and arriving at a broader societal marketing concept. We shall outline the implications of this development for productivity measurement.

TRADITIONAL MARKETING ORIENTATIONS

Marketing thought has been in constant evolution over time and in particular has broadened out significantly. Table 1 shows the distinguishing characteristics of the main phases of evolution, as well as summarizing the most important properties of the environment taken to determine the appropriate marketing orientation. The last column proposes an appropriate productivity concept. Essentially, Table 1 shows how the broadening of marketing thought creates a need for parallel extensions in productivity conceptualization. The first three orientations:
- the production orientation
- the selling concept orientation
- the marketing concept orientation
are here classified as traditional orientations.

Production Orientation

Production orientation prevailed throughout the period of industrialization in the Western world (and to some extent in the temporary scarcity situation after the second world war in Europe and Japan). As demand greatly exceeded supply, the main problem was to produce as much as possible. Production economies were achieved through product standardization and by mass production technology. Marketing activities were assumed to be of limited importance beyond mere physical distribution.

Since the supply of skilled manpower tended to constitute the main bottle-neck in production, the appropriate productivity concept related to labour productivity (physical production volume per unit of labour input). While the environment today is vastly different from that of the production orientation period, this traditional productivity concept has maintained a dominant position not only in the public debate, but also in empirical research.

Selling Concept Orientation

The selling concept emerged when supply started to catch up with demand. To keep up with growing competition, manufacturers had to invest in advertising and personal selling, and research gave most of its attention to the elements

TABLE 1

RELATIONSHIP BETWEEN STAGE IN MARKETING ORIENTATION
AND APPROPRIATE PRODUCTIVITY CONCEPT

STAGE IN MARKETING ORIENTATION	PROPERTIES OF THE ENVIRONMENT	EXTENSION OF MARKETING CONCEPT	APPROPRIATE PRODUCTIVITY MEASURE
Production Orientation	Early industrial society. Demand much greater than supply. Limited direct competition.		$\dfrac{\text{Production volume}}{\text{Labour input}}$
Selling Concept	Industrial society. Stable environment. Growing direct competition.	Extension of marketing mix from price and physical distribution to include also advertising and personal selling.	$\dfrac{\text{Sales volume}}{\text{Labour input}}$
Marketing Concept	Industrial society. Substantial direct competition. Growing indirect competition.	Extension to all elements of the marketing mix.	$\dfrac{\text{Economic value added}}{\text{Total factor input}}$
Broadened Marketing Concept	Late industrial society. Substantial indirect competition.	Extension of users from private (business) companies to all organizations.	$\dfrac{\text{Value added for customers}}{\text{Total factor input}}$
Generic Marketing Concept	Early post-industrial society. Recognized ecological and social limits to growth. Politicized environment.	Extension of target groups from customers to all stakeholder publics.	$\dfrac{\text{Value added for each stakeholder public}}{\text{Costs incurred by the respective stakeholder public}}$
Societal Marketing Concept	Post-industrial society. Emphasis on the quality of life.	Extensions from goals of short-term customer wants to long-term consumer and public welfare.	$\dfrac{\text{Total short- and long-term value added for each stakeholder public}}{\text{Total short- and long-term costs incurred by the respective stakeholder public.}}$

of the marketing mix. The key to marketing success according to this view was to standardize and boost promotional effort. Because it was no longer obvious whether all products produced would ultimately be bought, it was appropriate to replace production volume with sales volume as the numerator in the productivity ratio. Since most marketers offered more than one product for sale, it was also appropriate to express sales in dollars rather than in physical quantity.

Marketing Concept Orientation

The marketing concept (or rather the marketing management concept) was the practical response of American businessmen in the 1950s to what they felt was a change from a seller's to a buyer's market. The seller's insistence on promoting wrong or marginal products would not, it was maintained, lead to long-run profits. Therefore, the new concept claimed to shift the focus from the product and the needs of the seller to the needs and wants of the buyer. Gearing marketing to customer preferences called for market research and effective coordination of all elements of the marketing mix - price, product, distribution and promotion (Kotler, 1976).

Although in principle the new concept gave more attention to consumer preferences, consumers continued to be viewed instrumentally, as a means to the end of profit. The marketing concept view of the market process placed the sellers in an active role as the **subject,** while consumers played a reactive part as the **object.** It is perhaps no wonder that most research inspired by the marketing concept has focused on the way in which individual consumers make pre-purchase decisions in favour of certain brands.

The appropriate productivity criterion would seem to be the ratio of economic value to total factor input, (see Table 1).

As pointed out by Beckman (1969), total volume measures of productivity had the weakness of involving considerable duplication, and of confusing productive inputs with costs. Therefore, to get closer to the true economic value added, the cost of materials, supplies and contract work should be deducted from the selling value of the product.

The correct denominator of the productivity ratio implied by the marketing concept would seem to be total factor input (rather than labour input only) because of the capital requirements of effective large scale marketing.

MODERN MARKETING ORIENTATIONS

The three successive marketing orientations falling into the so-called modern group are:
- the broadened marketing concept orientation
- the generic marketing concept orientation
- the societal marketing concept orientation

Broadened Marketing Concept Orientation

The broadened marketing concept originated in a much discussed article published by Kotler and Levy (1969), which extended earlier notions developed by Wiebe (1951-52). Kotler and Levy argued that marketing behaviour is manifest in a wide range of situations beyond the conventional exchange of goods and services for money, such as in the activities of schools, police administration, trade unions, charities, presidential campaigns, etc. Hence, marketing thought should be extended to the activities of all organizations that could be said to have customers and products in the wider sense. This expansion is evidently a response to the growing importance of non-profit organizations competing both among themselves and, more indirectly, with profit organizations - for customers' money, time, attention, political support, etc. The application of marketing to social or non-profit-organizations has become increasingly important.

The extension of marketing thought from pure market transactions to all organization-client transactions, economic and non-economic, requires that the numerator in the productivity ratio should also be broadened - from economic value added to value added, (see Table 1). This raises new measurement problems since the volume of **market** transactions can no longer be used as a point of departure for estimating value added. For non-profit organizations special ways are needed of measuring the extent to which organizational objectives are met.

Generic Marketing Concept Orientation

Defending his broadened concept before critics, Kotler argued that its main weakness was not that it was too broad, but that it did not go far enough. In his proposal for further broadening, Kotler suggested that marketing should not be restricted to relations with clients or users only. Instead, marketing should be expanded so as to apply to relations with all "audiences" or "stakeholder" groups and not just consumers (Kotler, 1972).

Part of the background to this conceptual expansion is the politicization of business and organizational decision making, and the corresponding need for inside and outside lobbying (Arndt, 1979).

The existence of multiple "audiences" makes it difficult, if at all possible, to aggregate productivity into a uni-dimensional, weighted index. Instead, a multi-dimensional concept of productivity is needed involving a separate productivity ratio for each target group.

Societal Marketing Concept Orientation

Philip Kotler is also the architect of the last modern marketing concept. In the third edition of his popular marketing textbook, Kotler proposes that management should aim at "generating customer satisfaction and long-term consumer and public welfare as the key to satisfying organizational goals and responsibilites" (Kotler, 1976, p. 18).

This means that marketing programmes and products should not only offer consumers immediate satisfaction and be easily marketable, but also contribute to long-term consumer welfare. This view requires consumer research to break out of the narrow confines of information processing and shift to more fundamental, holistic aspects of consumer behaviour. More specifically, the societal marketing concept calls for an extension of consumer research from wants and demands to needs, from individual decisions to group processes, from pre-purchase decision-making to consumption and post-consumption activities, and from the purchase of non-durables to more comprehensive areas such as time utilisation, household management, consumer ways of life and consumption styles (Uusitalo, 1979). Even a normative consumer behaviour tradition is needed in marketing.

As discussed here, the changes introduced by the societal marketing concept relate mainly to the output or effect dimension. Long-term effects and externalities (unintended effects on third parties) must be taken into consideration. By recognizing the ecological and social limits to growth, this orientation questions the belief which has dominated economic thought since Adam Smith, namely that the motivation of self-interest, i.e. the pursuit of profits and benefits by business and consumers, would, through the invisible hand of the market, produce benefits for everybody. Such a view ignores the externalities produced by marketing activities. In the words of Gracco and Rostenne: "people today are discovering that air, water, time and privacy are scarce commodities...They are forced to accept the noise of neighbours' motorbikes, the polluted river created by the upstream papermill, the junk of discarded cars, the foul smell of passing automobiles, the exhaustion of natural resources" (Cracco and Rostenne, 1971, p. 27).

The implication is that the appropriate productivity measure should allow for externalities by adding to the directly incurred costs the costs of pollution, depletion of non-renewable resources, etc. On the other hand, social and ecological benefits not included in sales should be included in output.

The generic and societal marketing concepts would seem to imply a parallel global concept of productivity. One of the theoretical foundations for the global productivity concept is the so-called pluralistic view of the organization.

THE PLURALISTIC PARADIGM

The traditional notion of the firm cast management in the role of serving shareholder interests alone and using employees and customers as a means of earning profits. Modern notions, however, recognize that groups other than shareholders or owners are affected. In the pluralistic view, the organization is a political community of internal and external "stakeholder" groups. Each "stakeholder" group (labour, bankers, suppliers, distributors, consumers, local and national government, the general public, etc.) is at once **contributor** (by giving time, money, raw materials and fabricated parts, "legitimacy", etc.) and **claimant** (by receiving money, finished products, ego gratification, etc.). The interests of each "stakeholder" group are in part identical with, in part different from (sometimes even antithetical to) those of the firm, see Thorelli (1977) and Arndt (1979). Hence, this view places management in a political or broker function: it has to work out acceptable "exchange ratios" for the most important "stakeholder" groups.

Productivity research has in the past neglected the externalities of production and consumption. Hence, the exploitation of labour and the exhaustion of non-renewable natural resources appeared to contribute to higher productivity, since they were not included among the inputs or costs. Similarly, investments in improvement of working conditions or in anti-pollution have been viewed as costs only, with no corresponding output or benefit. The pluralistic paradigm implies that such externalities should be internalized. Both costs and benefits should be included in productivity measurement (Helgesen, 1978).

TOWARDS A GLOBAL PRODUCTIVITY CONCEPT

The pluralistic view of the organization means that the traditional uni-dimensional productivity measure is inadequate as a measure of total performance. Instead the productivity ratio of outputs to inputs should be calculated for each "stakeholder" group separately.

For the consuming public for instance, output may relate to both short-term and long-term satisfactions. The input or cost factor may include monetary expenditure on the product purchased, time needed for acquisition, usage and disposal, etc. as proposed many years ago by Hollander (1961). Perhaps data about consumer satisfaction and complaints could be used as a measure in this respect. For workers, output may consist of wages received, job satisfaction, social relationships, status, etc., while input comprises time, energy, loyalty, health etc. The appropriate statistics may include turnover analysis, job satisfaction rating, etc.

According to the multi-dimensional productivity concept, total productivity increases if one "stakeholder" group improves its productivity ratio and the ratio for no other group deteriorates. If the ratio for one group is improved, while the ratio for one or more other groups drops, the matter is more problematical. One solution would be to weight changes in the productivity ratio according to the power or the needs of the "stakeholder" groups in question.

OBSTACLES FACING THE BROADENED CONCEPTS

We should not overlook the formidable obstacles facing the implementation of the societal marketing and global productivity concepts.

Traditional forms of education will probably not suffice. The new concepts cannot be internalized until they have been built into management's reward and incentive system. As long as return on investment remains the dominant performance criterion, the extent of socially and environmentally responsible management behaviour is likely to remain insignificant.

A serious problem is that companies (or even nations) who are ecologically concerned may have difficulty competing with their ecologically more backward competitors. Hence, the modern version of "social dumping" (unfair competition from low-wage countries) may be termed "ecological dumping". The long-term solution to the problem may be global efforts with respect to the environment and effective multinational agreements. In the short run, special taxes and subsidies may serve to establish competitive parity.

CONCLUSIONS

This article has attempted to link the development of a global productivity concept proposal to the evolution of modern generic and societal marketing concepts. The traditional productivity concept was simple, objective, easily quantifiable and uni-dimensional. The concept proposed, on the other hand, is complex, subjective, partially qualitative, and multi-dimensional.

The new productivity concept presented here clearly needs more solid theoretical underpinning. It cannot be denied that the practical measurement problems are formidable. However, it is necessary to try to avoid Gresham's law of productivity measurement - whereby "bad" criteria tend to drive out the "good" ones. The emerging social accounting tradition may provide clues for solving the methodological problems.

If the new concept could be made operational, it might show that the current alleged stagnation in productivity is to some extent an artefact of measurement. Similarly, the seemingly impressive productivity advances in the "cowboy economy" of the past would perhaps evaporate if the true externalities were taken into account.

Even if the global concept could be developed successfully, it would in all likelihood **supplement** rather than **replace** the traditional concept of volume per unit of labour input. There will still be a need for the latter concept, for instance in comparative studies of "relative competitiveness" (comparing effectiveness or changes in effectiveness of competing marketing entities).

101

REFERENCES

Arndt, J. (1979). Toward a concept of domesticated markets. **Journal of Marketing, 43** (Fall), 69-75.

Barger, H. (1955). **Distribution's place in the American economy since 1869.** New York: National Bureau of Economic Research and Princeton University Press.

Bartels, R. (1962). **The development of marketing thought,** Homewood, Illinois: Richard D. Irwin.

Beckman, T.N. (1969). The value added concept as measurement output. In: B.M. Enis and K.K. Cox (Eds.), **Marketing classics,** pp. 37-47 Boston: Allyn and Bacon.

Bucklin, L.P. (1972). **Competition and evolution in the distributive trades.** Englewood Cliffs, New Jersey: Prentice-Hall.

Bucklin, L.P. (1978a). **Productivity in marketing.** Chicago: American Marketing Association.

Bucklin, L.P. (1978b). Research in productivity measurement for marketing decisions. In: J.N. Sheth (Ed.), **Research in marketing,** Vol. 1, pp. 1-22. Greenwich, Connecticut: JAI Press.

Bucklin, L.P. & Preston, L.E. (1973). Market activity, performance, and productivity. In: B.W. Becker & H. Becker (Eds.). In: **Combined proceedings 1973,** pp. 548-553. Chicago: American Association.

Cox, R., Goodman, C.S., & Fichandler, T.C. (1965). **Distribution in a high-level economy.** Englewood Cliffs, New Jersey: Prentice-Hall.

Cracco, E., & Rostenne, J. (1971). The socio-ecological product. **MSU Business Topics, 19** (Summer), 27-34.

Helgesen, T. (1978). **What is productivity?** Oslo: Norwegian Productivity Institute.

Hilger, M.T. (1978). Theories of the relationship between marketing and economic development: public policy implications. In: P.D. White & C.C. Slater (Eds.), MACRO-MARKETING: **Distributive Process from a Societal Perspective, An Elaboration of Issues,** pp. 333-349. Boulder, Colorado: Business Research Division, University of Colorado.

Hollander, S.C. (1961). Measuring the cost and value of marketing. **Business Topics,** 9 (Summer), 17-27.

Kotler, P. (1972). A generic concept of marketing. **Journal of Marketing, 36** (April), 46-54.

Kotler, P. (1976). **Marketing management,** Third Edition. Englewood Cliffs, New Jersey: Prentice-Hall.

Kotler, P., & Levy, S.J. (1969). Broadening the concept of marketing.

Journal of Marketing, 33 (January), 10-15.

Mark, J.A. (1971). Concepts and measures of productivity. In: **The meaning and measurement of productivity,** Bulletin 1714 of the Bureau of Labor Statistics. Washington, D.C.: U.S. Government Printing Office.

Sevin, C.H. (1975). **Marketing productivity analysis.** New York: McGraw-Hill.

Stewart, P.W., Dewhurst J.F., & Field, L. (1939). **Does distribution cost too much?** New York: The Twentieth Century Fund.

Thorelli, H.B. (1977). Organizational theory: an ecological view. In: H.B. Thorelli (Ed.), **Strategy + structure = performance.** Bloomington, Indiana: Indiana University Press.

Uusitalo, L. (1979). **Consumption style and way of life.** Helsinki: Helsinki School of Economics.

Wiebe, G. (1951-52). Merchandising commodities and citizenship on television. **Public Opinion Quarterly, 15** (Winter), 679-691.

INTERCOUNTRY COMPARISONS OF ENERGY CONSUMPTION PATTERNS: METHODOLOGY AND USEFULNESS

Lars Bergman [1]

1. INTRODUCTION

One hardly needs to consult international energy statistics in order to find out that the level of per capita energy consumption differs significantly between countries. Thus, while the level of per capita energy consumption was 8.35 t.o.e. (tons of oil equivalent) in the US in 1972, the corresponding figure for Sweden was 5. 31 and for Japan 2.90 (for India it was only 0.2). To some extent these differences are reduced if per capita income differences are taken into account. Thus, the use of energy per unit of GDP in 1972 was 1.48 t.o.e. per million US $ in the US, while it was 1.06 and 0.85 in Sweden and Japan respectively.

On the basis of figures such as these one is tempted to conclude that the American "life-style" or consumption pattern implies a higher level of per capita energy consumption than, for instance, the Swedish one. However, many structural factors may underlie intercountry differences in aggregated measures such as energy consumption per capita or per unit of GDP. In addition to income and price differences there are also a number of other factors, such as differences in climatic conditions, population density, area and natural resource endowment. The latter factor tends to be a major determinant of a country's specialization in international trade, and thus of the export and import of energy-intensive products, such as steel, paper and basic chemicals.

The purpose of this study is to analyze the relative importance of different structural factors in explaining international differences in energy consumption. This is done by presenting, and partly applying, a two step

---

[1] Stockholm School of Economics

approach to intercountry comparison of energy consumption patterns. The aim of the approach is to reveal which differences are due to basic differences in technology and "life-style", while disregarding differences due to structural factors, income levels and relative prices. The term "life-style" is here taken to represent all the international differences in per capita energy consumption which cannot be explained by differences in technology or the structural factors mentioned above.

In the first step, differences due to structural factors such as income, climate, intracountry travel distances and natural resource endowments are eliminated, while the aim of the second step, which can be carried out independently of the first, is to eliminate the impact of relative prices. The first step of the approach is illustrated by some numerical calculations, while the second step is only described in principle.

2. THE FIRST STEP: MODEL AND DATA

In the first step an input-output approach (Bergman et.al. 1980) is used. Although there is by now a vast literature on international comparisons of energy consumption patterns, the use of input-output methods is not very common. Instead most of these studies are based on engineering data about individual processes and activities.

The use of relatively aggregated input-ouput data, as opposed to various kinds of microdata, has its advantages and its disadvantages. The basic advantage is that the i/o model yields a more comprehensive measure of the "energy intensity" of a given activity than simple observations on the input of energy per unit of output; using the i/o model it is possible to incorporate the indirect use of energy (i.e., the energy used in the production of non-energy inputs) in the estimation of the energy intensity of a given process. The main disadvantage with available input-output statistics is the high level of aggregation, which tends to reduce the usefulness of the i/o model for characterization of the technology used in various processes.

The methodological approach used in the first step is very simple. Using the static Leontief model, the observed differences in per capita final energy consumption between two countries are broken down into a number of components. These components are then grouped so that energy consumption differences due to technological, consumption pattern or "life-style" and foreign trade factors can be distinguished.

The breakdown of observed energy consumption differences using input-output data was initially carried out by Strout in an unpublished work cited by Reardon (1973). A similar approach was later adopted by Reardon himself. Bergman (1977) carried the decomposition further, particularly by breaking down the final demand effects into a volume component and a composition component. In all these studies, the subject was the change in energy consumption over time in one country (U.S. and Sweden, respectively).

The basic model is the usual static Leontief model except that the energy sectors are treated as exogenous. That is, the quantities of total supply (domestic production plus imports minus exports) of three kinds of final energy are treated as primary resources, and the deliveries of intermediate inputs to the energy sectors are treated as part of domestic final demand. The energy input coefficients in the energy-using production sectors, as well as the energy deliveries to the final demand sectors, are converted to physical units - million tons of oil equivalent (mtoe) - while the remaining intersectoral flows are measured in monetary terms. The basic model can then be written:

$$X = aX + Y_D + Y_Z - M \tag{1}$$

$$E = \varepsilon X + E_D \equiv E_I + E_D \tag{2}$$

where

X	=	a vector of per capita gross production
Y_D	=	a vector of per capita domestic final demand
Y_Z	=	a vector of per capita exports
M	=	a vector of per capita imports
a	=	a matrix of input-output coefficients
E	=	total final energy consumption
E_I	=	final energy use in the production sectors (except the energy sector)
E_D	=	final energy use in the household and energy sectors

ε =   a vector of direct energy input coefficients ε_i.

If (1) is solved and the solution substituted into (2), one obtains:

$$E_I = \varepsilon(I - a)^{-1}[Y_D + Y_Z - M] \equiv e[Y_D + Y_Z - M] =$$ (3)

$$= eY_D + eY_Z - eM,$$

where

e = a vector of total (direct + indirect) energy input coefficients.

This is the formulation of the model which will be used in the following. It implies that the analysis is focused on energy use within the country and that imports are treated as perfect substitutes for domestic production in all sectors. This is certainly an extreme assumption but, for want of information on the substitutability of imports and domestic production, it is reasonable to employ the assumption which yields the least cumbersome formulae.

Using (3), the differences in per capita final energy consumption within the production system between two countries, 0 and 1, can be written:

$$\Delta E_I = E_I^1 - E_I^0 =$$

$$= (e^1 Y_D^1 - e^0 Y_D^0) + (e^1 Y_Z^1 - e^0 Y_Z^0) - (e^1 M^1 - e^0 M^0).$$ (4)

Next, define a new hypothetical demand vector $\hat{Y}_D$ such that:

$$\sum_i \hat{Y}_{Di} = \sum_i Y_{Di}^1 \text{ and } \frac{\hat{Y}_{Dj}}{\sum_i \hat{Y}_{Di}} = \frac{Y_{Dj}^0}{\sum_i Y_{Di}^0} \text{ , } j = 1,\ldots,n$$

One can say that $\hat{Y}_D^0$ has the same volume as Y_D^1 and the same composition as Y_D. Similarly, vectors $\hat{Y}_Z$ and $\hat{M}$ are defined for exports and imports.

Using these definitions, equation (4), after some manipulation, can be written as follows:

$$\Delta E_I = [(e^1 - e^0)(Y_D^1 + Y_Z^1 - M^1)] +$$

$$+ [e^0(Y_D^1 - \hat{Y}_D)] + [e^0(Y_Z^1 - \hat{Y}_Z)] - [e^0(M^1 - \hat{M})] + \qquad (5)$$

$$+ [e^0(\hat{Y}_D - Y_D^0)] + [e^0(\hat{Y}_Z - Y_Z^0)] - [e^0(\hat{M} - M^0)]$$

or

$$\Delta E_I = [(e^1 - e^0)(Y_D^0 + Y_Z^0 - M^0)] +$$

$$+ [e^1(Y_D^1 - \hat{Y}_D)] + [e^1(Y_Z^1 - \hat{Y}_Z)] - [e^1(M^1 - \hat{M})] + \qquad (6)$$

$$+ [e^1(\hat{Y}_D - Y_D^0)] + [e^1(\hat{Y}_Z - Y_Z^0)] - [e^1(\hat{M} - M^0)]$$

The difference between the two countries in final energy consumption in the household and government sectors, ΔE_D, can be broken down in the following way:

$$\Delta E_D = E_D^1 - E_D^0 = d^1 \bar{Y}_D^1 - d^0 \bar{Y}_D^0 \qquad (7)$$

where

$$\bar{Y}_D^k = \sum_i Y_{Di}^k \quad \text{and} \quad d^k = \frac{E_D^k}{\bar{Y}_D^k} \quad ; \quad k = 0,1$$

i.e., d^0 and d^1 represent the final energy consumption per unit of domestic final demand in countries 0 and 1 respectively. Similar to equation (4), equation (7) can be written:

$$\Delta E_D = d^1(\bar{Y}_D^1 - \bar{Y}_D^0) + \bar{Y}_D^0(d^1 - d^0) \tag{8}$$

or

$$\Delta E_D = (d^1 - d^0)\bar{Y}_D^1 + d^0(\bar{Y}_D^1 - \bar{Y}_D^0) \tag{9}$$

For computation, the respective averages of (5) with (6) and (8) with (9) are used. Thus the following decomposition of the difference in per capita final energy consumption between country 1 and country 0 is reached:

$$\underset{\text{TOT}}{\Delta E} = (e^1 - e^0)\,\frac{Y_D^1 + Y_Z^1 - M^1 + Y_D^0 + Y_Z^0 - M^0}{2} +$$

$$\text{I/O}$$

$$+ \underset{\text{DOM.COMP}}{\frac{e^1 + e^0}{2}(Y_D^1 - \hat{Y}_D)} + \underset{\text{EXP.COMP}}{\frac{e^1 + e^0}{2}(Y_Z^1 - \hat{Y}_Z)} - \underset{\text{IMP.COMP}}{\frac{e^1 + e^0}{2}(M^1 - \hat{M})} +$$

$$+ \underset{\text{DOM.VOL}}{\frac{e^1 + e^0}{2}(\hat{Y}_D - Y_D^0)} + \underset{\text{EXP.VOL}}{\frac{e^1 + e^0}{2}(\hat{Y}_Z - Y_Z^0)} - \underset{\text{IMP.VOL}}{\frac{e^1 + e^0}{2}(\hat{M} - M^0)} +$$

$$+ \underset{\text{DIR.INP}}{(d^1 - d^0)\frac{Y_D^1 + \bar{Y}_D^0}{2}} + \underset{\text{DIR.VOL}}{\frac{d^1 + d^0}{2}(\bar{Y}_D^1 - \bar{Y}_D^0)} \tag{10}$$

where

TOT	= Total difference in final energy consumption (DFEC)
I/O	= DFEC due to different input-output coefficients
DOM.COMP	= DFEC due to different composition of domestic final consumption
EXP.COMP	= DFEC due to different composition of exports
IMP.COMP	= DFEC due to different composition of total imports

DOM.VOL *

DIR.VOL	= DFEC due to different volume of domestic final consumption
EXP.VOL	= DFEC due to different volume of total exports
IMP.VOL	= DFEC due to different volume of total imports
DIR.INP	= DFEC due to different levels of direct final energy consumption per unit of domestic final consumption.

As equation (10) contains more components than are necessary for our purposes, some aggregation can be undertaken. In the following the analysis is focused on three components, of which two are aggregated. The I/O component is left as it stands in equation (10) and taken as a measure of the difference in final energy consumption due to technological factors. More specifically, the I/O component answers the question: "If the net final demand in country 1 and country 0 were aggregated, and each of the countries supplied half of the resulting demand for each commodity group, what would be the difference in energy consumption between the two countries?" Using this approach different processes receive different relative weights in the aggregate description of the technology, but the weights are the same for both countries.

The components DIR.INP and DOM.COMP both reflect differences in final energy consumption due to the composition of domestic final consumption (DIR.INP for energy, DOM.COMP for other goods and services). The other two components associated with domestic final consumption, DOM.VOL and DIR.VOL, represent a pure scaling of the use of energy. In other words, both price and income factors affecting the composition of domestic final demand are reflected in the components DOM.COMP and DIR.INP. In the following the sum of these components is referred to as differences due to "life-style". The life-style component (DIR.INP + DOM.COMP) answers the question: "If the volume of domestic final demands were the same in both countries, and both countries produced equal shares of the supply of all commodity groups, what would be the difference in

---

* Because $\hat{Y}_D$ has the same volume as Y_D^1 but the same composition as Y_D^0, DOM.VOL can be written

$$ \text{DOM.VOL} = \frac{e^1 + e^0}{2} (\hat{Y}_D - Y_D^0) = \frac{e^1 + e^0}{2} \frac{Y_D^0}{\bar{Y}_D^0} (\bar{Y}_D^1 - \bar{Y}_D^0), $$

i.e, it reflects the difference in the volume of domestic final demand. A similar transformation of EXP.VOL and IMP.VOL can be made to see that these components reflect the difference in the volume of exports and imports, respectively.

energy consumption due to the different composition of domestic final demand?" This component reflects differences in the consumption patterns due to relative prices and income levels as well as differences in preferences.

The third component of interest is defined by the four components in equation (10) related to foreign trade. In the following this aggregated component is denoted "Trade". The trade component (EXP.COMP + EXP.VOL - IMP.COMP - IMP.VOL) can be characterized in almost the same way as the life-style component: "If net foreign trade were the same in both countries, and both countries produced equal shares of the supply of all commodity groups, what would be the difference in energy consumption due to net foreign trade?" This component reflects differences in the pattern of comparative advantage, resulting from differences in resource endowments and other factors between the countries.

In order to estimate these components, i/o tables and energy consumption statistics for a given year are needed for the countries under study. For reasons explained in the following section, the numerical analysis was carried out for three countries: France, the Federal Republic of Germany (FRG) and the Netherlands. The i/o tables were taken from a collection of standardized input-output tables of ECE countries for years around 1965 (Economic Commission for Europe, 1977). There are two versions available, namely a 22 sector and a 45 sector version. The aggregated version was chosen for this study. The tables were normalized for population and converted to a common currency unit (DM) using hypothetical exchange rates in terms of purchasing power parity calculated by Kravis et.al. (1978). The final energy consumption data were taken from OECD (1976).

3. SOME COMPARISONS BETWEEN FRG, FRANCE AND THE NETHERLANDS

In order to select countries for the numerical analysis three basic criteria are applied. First, the selected countries should have approximately the same level of GDP per capita, because we want to identify cases where countries with approximately the same material standard of living differ significantly in terms of energy consumption patterns. Therefore, FRG, France and the Netherlands are reasonably good choices (see Table 1).

Secondly, in order to apply the approach described in the preceding section, comparable input-output tables should be available for at least one year. This is the case for FRG, France and the Netherlands (for 1965), but this criterion rules out the U.S. and Sweden, on which several studies in this field have been focused.

Whether the third criterion, namely that the countries should have approximately identical production functions, holds for the three countries is not easy to verify. However, it is reasonable to assume that labour skills and the stock of technological knowledge is about the same in countries like FRG, France and the Netherlands. Moreover, information on new technologies should be available at about the same time in these countries. Thus, the range of potential techniques facing investors should be approximately the same in the FRG, France and the Netherlands. However, due to different rates of economic growth, the share of relatively new capital in the total capital stock can be expected to be somewhat different in the three countries. The importance of this factor is difficult to evaluate, but assumed to be relatively minor.

Other factors affecting the production functions are climate and intracountry travel distances. The importance of these factors can be discussed in connection with the following two tables:

Table 1
GDP and final energy consumption indices 1965
for FRG, France and the Netherlands

	Per capita final energy consumption	GDP per capita (in terms of purchasing power parities)	Final energy consumption per unit of GDP
FRG	100	100	100
France	76	92	83
Netherlands	83	82	101

Sources:
See Tables 2 and 3.

Table 2
Climate and travel distance indicators
and adjusted per capita energy consumption indices
for FRG, France and the Netherlands

	Average no. of degree days	Area	Population density	Adjusted* per capita energy cons.
FRG	100	100	100	100
France	85	222	37	78
Netherlands	105	18	155	80

*
Final energy consumption minus energy use in the transportation sector and the use of fuels in the household and public service sectors, as given in the OECD energy balance sheets.

Sources:
For degree days: J. Darmstadter et al. (1977), How industrial societies use energy.
For area: International Road Federation (1970), World Road Statistics 1965-69.
For population and energy consumption: see Tables 2 and 3

Table 1 contains some basic economic and energy consumption data. It reveals non-negligible differences between the countries in terms of final energy consumption per capita. To some extent these differences coincide with the differences in terms of GDP per capita. Thus, on the basis of Table 1 and adopting a popular way of reasoning, FRG and the Netherlands are equally "inefficient" in their utilization of energy, and both countries should learn from the more "energy efficient" France. However, "structural" factors can hide differences more relevant for energy conservation policy. Thus, on the basis of Table 1, no "energy efficiency" ranking can be made. Neither can it be ruled out that FRG and the Netherlands differ significantly in terms of efficiency of energy utilization, in spite of their similarity in terms of final energy consumption per unit of GDP.

Table 2 contains some data about climate and intracountry travel distances. The climatic factors can be reasonably well represented by the average number of degree days. Intracountry travel distances should depend on both the area of the country and the population density, but it is difficult to know exactly how. One could perhaps infer from Table 2 that the intercountry differences in final energy consumption per unit of GDP can be explained entirely by the differences in the average number of degree days. That, of course, is not the case. If final energy consumption is reduced by the amount of energy used in the transportation sector and all fuels used by the household and public service sectors, the remaining differences should be approximately net of energy used for transportation and heating purposes. As can be seen in Table 2 (the column "Adjusted per capita energy consumption"), such an operation leaves the intercountry differences in final energy consumption almost unaffected. Thus one can conclude that climatic factors and intracountry travel distances do not explain a substantial share of per capita final energy consumption differences between FRG, France and the Netherlands.

Next we turn to the application of the decomposition formula. The main results are summarized in Tables 3, 4 and 5. The first column contains estimates of the total difference in per capita final energy consumption (the component TOT in equation (10)). In the second, the difference in per capita final energy consumption is expressed as a ratio of the average level of per capita final energy consumption (for each energy form separately and for all forms together) in the two countries. According to this measure, it can be seen that the countries differ more in the consumption of individual kinds of energy than in terms of total per capita final energy consumption.

In columns (3) - (6) the results obtained from the application of equation (10) in Section 3 are presented. The differences due to each of the components "Technology", "Life-style" and "Trade" (as defined on p. 108-9) as well as the sum of the first two, are expressed as ratios of the total difference in per capita final energy consumption. If the value for "Technology" or "Life-style" is close to or greater than one, it is reasonable to conclude that important differences in energy consumption patterns are hidden by various "structural" factors.

As can be seen in the tables, there are a few cases where the absolute value of an individual component is significantly greater than the total difference. In particular, the Netherlands seem to have a technology which uses liquid fuels much more intensively than the technologies used in France and FRG. It is interesting to note that although FRG and the Netherlands are quite similar in terms of final energy consumption per unit of GDP, the energy intensities of the technologies used in the two countries are quite different.

114

Using the product of the figures in column (2) and the figure in one of columns (3), (4), (5) or (6) as a measure of the relative "importance" of the various components, it turns out that the "Trade" component in all the comparisons is smaller than 7.5 % of the average level of consumption of the fuel in question in the two countries under comparison. France seems to have the most energy intensive "life-style" of the three countries, although the Netherlands is the most electricity intensive country from this point of view. However, the differences between the countries in terms of the "Life-style" component are in most cases quite small.

Generally the "Technology" component appears to be quantitatively the most important one. In terms of the technology component FRG and France are rather similar, but both countries use technologies which, from an energy point of view, differ significantly from the technology used in the Netherlands. However, it should be noted that the ranking of the three countries on the basis of the aggregated "Technology" component is the same as the ranking based on final energy consumption per unit of GDP; the Netherlands is the most energy intensive country followed by FRG and France. In terms of final energy consumption per capita, however, FRG is the most energy intensive country in the sample, followed by the Netherlands and then France (see Table 1).

TABLE 3. A decomposition of the difference in per capita final energy consumption between FRG and the Netherlands (1965)

	1) ΔE	$\dfrac{2\,\Delta E}{E^0 + E^1}$	2) Technology+ Life-style $\dfrac{}{\Delta E}$	2) Technology $\dfrac{}{\Delta E}$	2) Life-style $\dfrac{}{\Delta E}$	2) Trade $\dfrac{}{\Delta E}$
	(1)	(2)	(3)=(4)+(5)	(4)	(5)	(6)
Gas and Solid Fuels	435.8	.583	.626 *	.556 *	.070	.044
Liquid Fuels	-118.5	.101	-2.894 *	-2.965 *	-.071	-.089
Electricity	61.9	.355	.228 *	.743 *	-.515 *	.208
Total	379.2	.181	-.146	-.167	.021	.057

1) $\Delta E = E_{FRG} - E_{NETH}$

2) See Equations (10) and Section 3
   for the definition of the components

*___ = (2) x (absolute value in col. (3),(4),(5) or (6)) $\geq$ .300
*---- = (2) x (absolute value in col. (3),(4),(5) or (6)) > .150 but < .300
*..... = (2) x (absolute value in col. (3),(4),(5) or (6)) $\geq$ .075 but < .150

TABLE 4. A decomposition of the differences in per capita
final energy consumption between the Netherlands
and France (1965)

	1) ΔE	$\dfrac{2 \Delta E}{E^0 + E^1}$	2) Technology+ Life-style $\overline{\Delta E}$	2) Technology $\overline{\Delta E}$	2) Life-style $\overline{\Delta E}$	2) Trade $\overline{\Delta E}$
	(1)	(2)	(3)=(4)+(5)	(4)	(5)	(6)
Gas and Solid Fuels	-195.4	.315	-1.038*	-.777* ------	-.261	-.136
Liquid Fuels	362.3	.343	.839* ------	.970*	-.131	.022
Electricity	-12.3	.082	1.000*	-1.789* -------	.789	-.650
Total	154.6	.085	.574	1.148	-.574	-.171

1) $\Delta E = E_{NETH} - E_{FRANCE}$

2) See Table 3

* See Table 3

TABLE 5. A decomposition of the difference in per capita
final energy consumption between FRG and France (1965)

	1) ΔE	$\dfrac{2\,\Delta E}{E^0 + E^1}$	2) Technology+ Life-style ΔE	2) Technology ΔE	2) Life-style ΔE	2) Trade ΔE
	(1)	(2)	(3)=(4)+(5)	(4)	(5)	(6)
Gas and Solid Fuels	240.4	.287	.100	.204	-.104	.035
Liquid Fuels	243.8	.490	-.061	.114	-.175*	.045
Electricity	49.7	.276	.035	.435*	-.400*	.058
Total	533.8	.265	.021	.185	-.164	.042

1) $\Delta E = E_{FRG} - E_{FRANCE}$

2) See Table 3

*   See Table 3

118

Table 6 gives some additional information about intercountry differences in energy consumption due to "life-style" factors.

Table 6

Pairwise country comparisons of "Life-style" differences in energy consumption

	DIR.INP	+	DOM.COMP =	Life-style
France-FRG	84.71		2.33	87.04
France-Netherlands	102.95		-14.15	88.80
FRG-Netherlands	30.30		-22.45	7.85

$$\text{DIR.INP} = \frac{Y_D^1 + Y_D^0}{2} (d^1 - d^0) \quad ; \text{DOM.COMP} = \frac{e^1 + e^0}{2} (\hat{Y} - Y_D^1).$$

The table clearly indicates that the commodity composition of final demand (excluding direct energy consumption) in France and FRG is such that the component DOM.COMP. is negligible. Moreover, in terms of that component, the Netherlands turn out to have the most energy intensive consumption pattern. However, when the direct consumption of energy, the component DIR.INP., is taken into account, France seems to have the most energy intensive life-style. Thus, even though France has the lowest use of energy per capita, and per unit of GDP, of the three countries, the French consumption pattern, adjusted for various "structural" and technology factors, seems to require more energy than the consumption patterns in FRG and the Netherlands.

4. THE SECOND STEP: INTERPRETATION OF THE RESULTS

So far we can conclude that domestic consumption patterns differ between countries with approximately the same per capita income levels in such a way that intercountry differences in energy consumption levels per capita emerge. The question, then, is how these results can be inerpreted: Do these differences result from basic "life-style" factors, or are they only a reflection of intercountry differences in relative prices? Clearly it is very difficult, or impossible, to give definite answers to questions such as these. However, some insight can be gained by means of price data and economic theory.

The starting point is Samuelson's axiom of revealed preferences
(Deaton-Mullbauer, 1980). Consider the following example, illustrating the
situation of an individual consumer. Given the budget A^oB^o (see Figure
1 below) the consumer has chosen the combination q^o of the commodities
q_1 and q_2. An increase of the price of q_2 shifts the budget line to
A^bB^1. Suppose that the consumer is fully compensated for the higher
price of q_2, i.e. that he is faced with the budget line A*B* which means
that he can continue to consume the combination q^o. In this situation the
axiom tells us that the consumer will not choose a bundle on the segment
q^oB^*. All points on that segment were feasible initially, but q^o was
revealed to be preferred to each one of these bundles. Thus, if anything, a
compensated increase in the price of a given commodity will lead to a
decrease of the demand for that commodity.

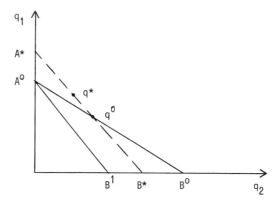

Figure 1

Assume that q* is the preferred bundle in the new situation. It follows that if
q* differs from q^o (as in Figure 1), it was not feasible in the initial
situation, i.e. $\Sigma p_k^o q_k^* \geq \Sigma p_k^o q_k^o$, where p_k^o are the prices
corresponding to A^oB^o. Since q* and q^o are both on A*B* (reflecting
the prices p_k^1), it further holds that $\Sigma p_k^1 q_k^* = \Sigma p_k^o q_k^o$.
Combination of these expressions yields

$$\sum_k (p_k^1 - p_k^o)(q_k^* - q_k^o) \leq 0$$

These ideas can in some cases be used to reject the hypothesis that households generally have the same preferences in two different countries. Assume that the prices in one country, expressed in some common international currency unit, are represented by the vector p^o, while the (comparable) prices in another country are represented by the vector p^1. The actual consumption patterns are given by the vectors q^1 and q^* respectively. Assume furthermore that $p^1 q^1 = p^1 q^o$, i.e. that in one of the countries the commodity bundle actually bought in the other country is feasible. If, under these conditions, equation (11) is violated, one can reject the hypothesis that intercountry consumption pattern differences only reflect differences in relative prices.

If a test of this kind is to be carried out in practice, both conceptual and empirical problems are encountered. In general these problems are aggregation problems and problems of measurement. Commodity groups with the same classification in two countries may, after all, not contain the same type of products in the same proportions. Reasonable price indices may be difficult to identify, and income distribution differences may make all comparisons difficult to interpret on the basis of demand theory.

However, if these problems are not attacked, international comparisons of energy consumption patterns will not be of much use. The comparisons may very well reveal a lot of interesting differences between countries, but the policy implications of the findings will be unclear.

5. CONCLUDING REMARKS

On the surface, intercountry comparison of per capita energy consumption patterns seems to be an efficient way of demonstrating the possiblility of maintaining a certain material standard of living at a variety of energy consumption levels. It is efficient because real examples tend to be much more convincing than results obtained with simulation models and related methods. However, the intercountry differences in per capita energy consumption which can be observed do not only reflect differences between countries in terms of the efficiency of energy utilization. They may also reflect various structural factors such as differences in climate, population density, travel distances and natural resource endowments.

In this study a method for adjusting observed intercountry energy consumption differences has been presented and applied in a three-country comparison. The results indicate that a significant part of the observed differences can be explained by structural factors such as those mentioned above. Of the remaining differences a significant share can be explained by differences in the technology used in different countries. The remaining, unexplained differences can be interpreted in one of the following two ways.

If they essentially reflect differences in income levels and relative prices, intercountry comparisons of energy consumption patterns primarily indicate the long run price and income elasticities which, in that case, are reasonably applicable in most countries. In other words, such studies give energy policy makers an indication of the long run effects of energy policy measures working primarily through the price system.

If, on the other hand, the observed differences in energy consumption patterns largely reflect "life-style" differences which cannot be explained by income or price differences or other structural factors, the main role of international comparisons in this field is to give real examples of alternative "life-styles" to the public as well as to energy policy makers. Such studies might stimulate changes in attitudes rather than in prices. As was mentioned above, this is the role often assigned to intercountry comparisons of per capital energy patterns. The analysis in this study should demonstrate that a considerable amount of additional analysis is needed before observed intercountry differences in energy consumption can be interpreted along these lines.

REFERENCES

Bergman, L. (1977), **Energy and Economic Growth in Sweden,** Economic Research Institute, Stockholm School of Economics, Stockholm

Bergman, L., Clementz, C., Hoelzl, A. (1980), An Input-output Approach to the Analysis of Intercountry Differences in Per Capita Energy Consumption, WP-80-03, IIASA, Laxenburg, Austria

Darmstadter et al. (1977), **How industrial societies use energy,** RfF, John Hopkins University Press, Baltimore

Deaton, A., Muellbauer, J. (1980), **Economics and Consumer Behaviour,** Cambridge University Press

Griffin, J.M. (1976), **Energy input-ouput modelling: problems and prospects,** Centre for Energy Systems, General Electric Co., Washington, D.C.

Kravis, I. et al. (1978), "Real GDP per capita for more than one hundred countries", **Economic Journal,** 88

Reardon, W.A. (1973), "Input-output analysis of U.S. energy consumption", in Searl, M.F., **Energy Modeling,** RfF, WP-EN-1, Washington, D.C.

Economic Commission for Europe (1977), "Standardized input-output tables of EEC countries for years around 1965", **Statistical Standards and Studies (30),** United Nations, New York

OECD (1976), **Energy balances of OECD countries 1960 - 74,** Paris

United Nations (1975), **Demographic Yearbook 1974,** New York

United Nations (1978), **Yearbook of National Account Statistics 1976,** New York

123

ENVIRONMENTAL IMPACTS OF CHANGES IN CONSUMPTION STYLE

Liisa Uusitalo [1]

INTRODUCTION

There are several problems connected with the ecological effects of private consumption that deserve attention. In the past, several writers have discussed the necessity of striving for more "responsible consumption". There have been attempts to find out how ecological requirements could be reflected in marketing strategy or product policy and there have been endeavours to determine the characteristics of ecologically or socially responsible consumers. Some attention has also been paid to ecological concern as a motive in product or brand choice.

In empirical research, environmental problems related to household behaviour have been treated mainly at the micro-level. It is believed that factors on the personal level are important when planning behavioural change. A broad data base evidently exists concerning both individual environmental attitudes and individual behavioural changes in response to given environmental policy measures. In contrast, there is a lack of empirical data and research on the environmental impacts of more macro-level aspects of consumption behaviour and their social background.

The purely economic approach has been most conspicuous in the study of ecological destruction in society (e.g. pollution caused by the production sector). However, difficulties exist in applying this approach to consumption. When consumption externalities (e.g. environmental damages) emerge as a result of consumption choices, it can be difficult to create " markets" for environmental concern by using only economic incentives. Often no clear property rights can be established or, if they are established (e.g. as resting

1 The Helsinki School of Economics. Visiting research fellow at the International Institute for Environment and Society, Berlin, 1979 - 80

with the government), it is still difficult to control violation against them. Economic incentives may prove insufficient too when price elasticity is low or no clear price consciousness exists. Furthermore, the use of economic incentives is often undesirable because of their regressive distributional effects.

The economic theory of externalities therefore needs to be supplemented by theories that allow for the interdependence of people's choices as well as the social and institutional background of behaviour. Consequently, one can suggest that ecologically relevant behaviour has to be related to **dominant social and cultural patterns of behaviour** (ways of life, consumption styles), rather than being considered in terms of consumers' independent, individual choices. The first task, then, is to identify those elements in these behaviour patterns which are ecologically relevant, in order to be able either to reinforce them or to substitute them with other types of behaviour.

In previous studies of environmental impacts of household behaviour, especially those concerning energy consumption, it has often been claimed that life-style factors play an important part and may even prove to be more efficient explanatory variables than socioeconomic or demographic background (e.g., Schipper & Ketoff, 1980; Bergman, Clemens & Hoelzl, 1979). However, "lifestyle" has also often been treated as a "waste basket" or "catch-all" class, including a variety of variables which have not been accounted for by other predictor classes. That is, the term 'life-style' usually refers to various activities and/or situations within households - e.g., indoor temperature, energy-saving practices, intensity of use of household appliance and many other (usually unspecified) things.

This paper attempts to produce some hypotheses concerning the effects of life-style factors. The term 'life-style' is here understood as a holistic concept referring to a "whole" class of activities and preferences depending on people's personal, social and institutional background.

The major differences in life-style are here measured primarily with the help of two sorts of indicators: (1) consumption patterns and (2) time allocation patterns. Hence, the use of the term **'consumption style'** is preferred to 'life-style' or 'way of life', the latter being somewhat broader concepts.

125

Consumption style is understood to be an intervening variable between the structural and institutional changes in society and households' environmentally relevant behaviour. Therefore, attention will be given to structural factors underlying various consumption style properties (see Figure 1). The term 'environmental or ecological impacts' will refer primarily to the amount and composition of households' energy consumption and household waste. Other environmental impacts relating to household behaviour will only be touched upon superficially.

Figure 1. <u>Basic hypothetical model of the ecological</u>
         <u>impacts of consumption styles</u>

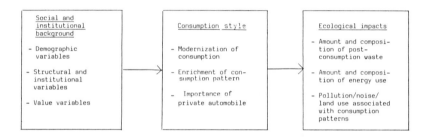

First, some general changes in consumption styles and their social background will be discussed. (The classification of these consumption style changes is based on earlier empirical studies by the author.) Following this preliminary discussion, some of the implications of these changes for the environment will be presented, using international empirical data to exemplify the hypothetical relationships between consumption style and environmental impacts.

DATA

The data have been extracted from several secondary sources and some have been compiled by the author. The primary purpose was to identify intercountry differences among the most important EEC countries (and in some cases OECD countries), or to identify differences over time within a single country where the necessary comparative data were not available. As the analysis used a rather wide range of variables, considerable difficulties emerged not only in collecting data, but also in converting them into a form suitable for comparison. (Similar difficulties in the collection of data on energy consumption have already been pointed out, e.g., by Hirst, 1979 and by Schipper, 1979.) In many cases - especially those concerning household waste statistics - the data consist of only very rough and often unreliable approximations. In this preliminary paper, the data are presented primarily in a descriptive manner. The application of multivariate methods has not been attempted at this point in the analysis.

GENERAL TRENDS IN CONSUMPTION STYLES

Modernization of Life

The general trend towards modernization in consumption and time-use patterns is best indicated by the increased share of expenditure on **mass-produced products and services** as opposed to the time-old tradition of **home production of commodities.** Because most of the main commodity expenditure groups include items which themselves indicate a modernized consumption pattern, it is difficult to demonstrate this trend empirically without the help of very detailed expenditure data. In a previous cross-sectional study of consumption patterns (Uusitalo, 1979), restaurant and cafe services, alcoholic beverages, and pre-prepared, processed foods in particular seemed to indicate a modernized way of life, while a high budget share for food items like flour and grain (which are needed in the home production of food) indicated a traditional consumption pattern.

With respect to time allocation, modernization was indicated by the decreasing share of time spent on housework and the increased amount of time spent in restaurants. Two further trends in modernization can be differentiated: first, the trend towards **career orientation** and away from home-production activities, and secondly, the trend towards a stronger **market-efficiency orientation** (as indicated by, e.g., the purchase of time-saving products and services) and away from the expressive life-style which allows an individual to enjoy "non-effective" time use for various activities (Uusitalo 1980).

However, the analysis of consumption patterns also led to identification of a slight reverse trend within some subgroups of the population, namely a trend towards a **neo-traditional form** of home production. "Neo-traditional consumers" are those households for whom home production has become a consciously preferred expressive activity. (This group often includes well-educated, white collar families enjoying a high level of household technology.) They give higher priority to expressive life-values than to efficiency orientation in terms of time use.

The trend towards neo-traditional consumption is often associated with a tendency towards **privatization** - that is, emphasis on activities within the nuclear family rather than those that entail participation in a broader social or political context. A privatized way of life implies a psychological feeling of independence from the outside world. Recreational and household needs are satisfied with the help of personal initiative, personal methods and personal equipment. In some cases, however, this may lead to an overemphasis on the acquisition of material goods considered to be in the common family interest.

In a cross-sectional study on an intracountry basis, modernization was best explained in terms of socioeconomic status (having a nonagricultural occupation), age (being young), and living area (urban). This implies certain structural changes in society whereby factors such as urbanization, changes in the occupation structure and women's increased role in the labour force may underlie modernized consumption. Changes in mass-production and distribution technology are necessary prerequisites for values changes in favour of a modernized consumption pattern.

Enrichment and Variety of Consumption

The second major trend in consumption styles is the enrichment of consumption and time-use "baskets". It is closely related to such background factors as socioeconomic status (white collar), education level and income. A high standard of housing and a large quantity of consumer durables are correlated with rich consumption baskets. The increase in income and educational level has been accompanied by an increase in the total number of households due to an increase in the number of one- and two-person families. This, in turn, has added to the total demand for e.g. household durables.

The enrichment of consumption patterns is probably best indicated by the high budget shares for discretionary spending (recreation, culture and education, furniture and decorative household items, novelty foods-gourmet cuisine) and in some cases by a high share of expenditure on clothing, medical and other personal care services. Usually, enrichment of consumption is further indicated by a low budget share for "necessities", of which total food expenditure is still a common measure. However, enrichment and improved quality also occur in expenditure on food.

In time allocation patterns an analogous trend (towards wider variety) can be observed. The trend is away from providing the necessities of life and towards satisfying either **individual desires** or towards **self-actualizing activities.** Which of these two paths of enrichment will become dominant depends greatly on which values - individual or collective ones - are emphasized more in society (Uusitalo 1980a).

In a cross-sectional study it was found that a wide variety in the consumption basket correlated with a many-sided and active use of time (cultural activities, associations/clubs, active sports) (Uusitalo 1979a). Thus, enriched consumption and leisure patterns are found together in the same households.

Private Automobile Use

The third of the basic, major changes in consumption styles has occurred within the mode of transportation, which has come to be dominated more and more by the private automobile. This general trend seems to be universal - social system notwithstanding - although taxation and import restrictions in some countries have decelerated it somewhat. Intracountry differences in the preference for private automobile usage also seem to be to a great extent independent of any underlying factors, with the exception of income, which determines the quality and the point of acquisition of the first car.

Even if the use of the private automobile is common to all countries, it may still be the case that great differences exist in the intensity of automobile use (kilometres driven per car per year) or in the effectiveness of car use (reflected in the passenger kilometres driven). The size of the automobile is also a typical "lifestyle" variable with great intra- and intercountry variations.

ENVIRONMENTAL IMPACTS

Impacts of Modernization

Probably the single most important environmental impact of modernization
(the increased use of mass-produced goods and sevices) is the increasing amount
of post-consumption waste. The more modernized and richer the country, the
higher the total per capita amount of household waste. In the 1970s, the yearly
amount of household waste was about 600 kilograms per capita in the USA,
and about 250 to 350 kilograms per capita in Western Europe.

Table 1. Composition of household waste by type of material
(weight % of total househod waste)

Country and year	USA 1971	USA 1975	FRG 1966	FRG 1970	Belgium 1966	Belgium 1973	France 1966	France 1975	UK 1966	UK 1973	Italy 1975
Glass	9	10	9	15-17	3	6	4	2-8	5-8	10	3
Organic	5		21		23		24		10-15		
- Wood	4	4								5	
- Vegetable matter+	14	38++		10-15		19		15-30		18	38
Minerals		2		10-36		18		10-20		19	4
-Ash			30		48		24		30-40		
Metals			5	3-6	2-3		4-5	2-6	5-8	10	7
- Ferrous	7	9		2-5		3-4					
- Non-ferrous	2	1		1							
Synthetic materials, e.g., plastics	1	4		3-5		5-6		2-6		1-2	7
Paper	55	29	19	30-40	20	28	30	20-40	25-30	33	29
Textiles, leather and rubber		5						1-6		3-4	6
Other	3		15	3-6	14				5-10		

+ Food and yard/garden waste

++ 18 % food waste plus 20 %
   yard/garden waste

Sources: Vogel, 1978; Langer and Stief, 1978;
         Resource recovery and waste reduction, 1977

The composition of household waste varies to some extent between countries. However, there is general tendency for the amount of **paper** and **glass** waste to increase in direct proportion to urbanization and income increases. (15 % of the paper in the USA (1975 figures) and 30 - 40 % of the paper in the FRG (1978 figures) is recycled. However, the majority of this recycled material does **not** come from households, but rather from commercial sources. Of glass, only 3 - 10 % is recycled.)

A third and important component of household waste is organic or vegetable matter, which includes both **food waste** and yard or garden waste. In the USA, for example, this share increased steadily during the 1970s. The share of metals and synthetic materials in household waste has also been on the increase in all countries (see Table 1).

In national studies, it was found that both the total amount of waste and its composition vary according to the size of the urban centre from which it originates (e.g. Materialen zum Abfallwirtschaftsprogramm, 1979). The relative amounts of glass and paper waste increase most rapidly along with the size of the city.

Table 2. Product composition of household waste, USA, 1975

	Million tons	Percentage of total weight
Newspapers, books, magazines	9.8	7.7
Containers and packaging materials	41.7	32.5
Major household appliances	2.3	1.8
Furniture, furnishings	3.4	2.7
Clothing and footwear	1.3	1.0
Other	18.9	14.7
NON-EDIBLE PRODUCTS TOTAL	77.5	60.4
Food waste	22.8	17.8
TOTAL PRODUCT WASTE	100.3	78.2
Yard and miscellaneous waste	27.9	21.8
GRAND TOTAL	128.2 m.tons	100.0 %

Source: Resource recovery and waste reduction, 1977

A very remarkable share of a modernized household's solid waste has its origin in **container and packaging products**. Table 2 gives a breakdown of the product composition of household solid waste in the USA. Container and packaging waste alone constitute one third of total solid waste by weight. Measured by volume, they represent an even more sizeable share - usually about one half of total waste volume (e.g., Schönfeld, 1978). Within the packaging waste category, paper and glass are still the two most dominant materials, but during the past twenty years there has been rapid growth in the quantities of plastic and aluminium packaging containers. Table 3 shows the importance of packaging material consumption relative to total material consumption with respect to paper, glass, plastic and aluminium. (The figures in this table also include those for packaging outside the consumer product sector.) About 50 % of paper consumption, 75 % of glass consumption and 30 % of plastic consumption is accounted for by packaging.

Table 3. Packaging-material consumption relative to total material consumption, USA, 1971

Type of material	Consumption Packaging (1,000 tons)	Total (1,000 tons)	Packaging as a percent of total consumption
Paper	27,700	58,652	47,2
Glass	11,100	14,900	74,5
Steel	7,255	87,038	8,3
Plastic	2,900	10,000	29,0
Aluminum	757	5,074	14,1

Source: Goddard, 1976

An interesting trend in "modernization" is shown in Table 4. While the absolute **product consumption** of dairy products, cereals and flour, and produce has **decreased**, the amount of **packaging consumption** within the same product classes has **increased**. Even the traditional households - those families who prefer to buy basic foodstuffs and prepare their food themselves - are no longer receiving their basic products without packaging.

Table 4. Food consumption relative to packaging consumption, USA, 1958-70

Type of product	Consumption (pounds per capita) 1958	1970	Change, 1958-70 (percent)
Dairy			
- Product consumption	398.0	354.0	-11.1
- Package consumption	10.6	13.3	25.5
Cereals, flour and related products			
- Product consumption	150.0	140.0	-6.0
- Package consumption	.8	.9	12.5
Produce (fresh fruit, vegetables)			
- Product consumption	90.2	80.0	-11.3
- Package consumption	5.3	7.3	37.7

Source: Goddard, 1976

In modern households using pre-prepared - e.g., frozen or canned - food, there will be a far greater amount of packaging to be thrown away. The increased consumption of alcoholic and other beverages among those households exhibiting a modernized consumption style contributes further to the problem of waste. In addition, pre-prepared food products are perhaps more readily discarded than are their home-production counterparts. Hence, modernized households will have larger quantities of food waste than traditional households.

Existing systems of recycling may have a great deal of influence on the type of litter that finally emerges from households. For example, the USA has a very high percentage of beverage container litter as compared to other countries whose returnable bottle systems are more widespread and/or more efficient. In addition to the waste/disposal aspect of the various types of containers, some other effects have been considered. For example, the OECD has calculated the pollution and energy impacts of different beverage containers (Beverage Containers, 1978).

A modernized consumption style does not necessarily imply only negative external consequences however. Urban living with its multiple dwelling houses and use of collective services (e.g., in the transportation sector) usually has an **economies-of-scale advantage,** especially in the area of **energy** consumption. Moreover, although the ownership of durables is just as high for present-day modern urban families as it is for traditional (rural) or neo-traditional (often suburban) families, the **intensity** of use of these durables may be somewhat reduced due to an increased interest of modern families in activities outside the home (Uusitalo, 1979c and 1980b).

Impacts of Enrichment in Consumption

Enrichment of consumption baskets contributes very much to the growth of **household waste** (as described above). In particular, discarded household items, including clothing, textiles and food waste, will increase.

The increased variety of consumption related for instance to size and standard of housing, residential pattern (e.g. number of single-family dwellings), quantity of durables owned, large recreational items and second homes is, however, primarily reflected in the households' use of **residential**

energy. Increased needs for comfort and satisfaction of newly developed desires in all spheres of life usually have an effect on direct or indirect energy use (where indirect energy means energy used to produce specific goods and services). During the 1970s, the share of residential energy in total final energy remained the same (i.e., 25 - 35 % of total end-energy use). Thus, the growth of residental energy use was as rapid as the growth of total energy use throughout the decade.

Table 5. Comparison between income and absolute residential energy consumption per capita in some countries (TOE)

	Energy price index for 1974 (USA, 1974 = 100)	Residential energy consumption					Income (total private consumption per capita in purchasing power parities)			
		1974	1975	1976	1977	1978	1974	1975	1976	1977
USA	1.16	1.480	1.408	1.534	1.555	1.595	--	--	--	--
FRG	2.66	1.042	1.028	0.863	0.875	0.931	2533	2994	3444	3845
Belgium	1.79	1.111	1.167	0.919	0.934	0.976	2476	2775	3219	3550
France	1.82	0.788	0.746	0.746	0.753	0.782	2566	2966	3399	3766
NL	1.34	0.988	1.066	1.170	1.071	1.077	2267	2606	2933	3291
UK	1.63	0.634	0.628	0.620	0.641	0.653	2194	2422	2693	2951
Italy	2.30	0.489	0.504	0.532	0.489	0.524	1830	2071	2335	2534

Ranking of countries according to residential energy consumption (1976)	Ranking of countries according to ownership of durables (1976)	Ranking of countries according to energy costs (1974)	Ranking of countries by private per capita consumption in US dollars (1974)
USA	USA	FRG	USA
NL	FRG	ITA	FRG
BEL	NL	FRA	BEL
FRG	BEL/FRA	BEL	FRA
FRA		UK	NL
UK	UK	NL	UK
ITA	ITA	USA	ITA

Sources: Energy balances of OECD countries; Pindyck, 1979; Jahresgutachten 1979-80 des sachverständigen rates zur Begutachtung der gesamtwirtsachaflichen Entwicklung, 1980

The ranking order of countries according to their per capita residential energy consumption (see Table 5) is the same as their ranking order according to saturation rates of household durables. (The sole exception to this is the Federal Republic of Germany, which ranks lower on the energy consumption scale than on the ownership-of-durables scale. This is undoubtedly due to the higher energy costs in West Germany, where the increase in real fuel and lighting prices from 1974 to 1978 was higher than in the other countries mentioned.) When comparing energy consumption with income level, France, for instance, seems to have lower residential energy consumption than the Netherlands or West Germany. It was previously found that, while France is the least energy-intensive with respect to production technology, it is the most energy-intensive of the three countries with respect to 'life-style' (Bergman et al., 1979). The cause of this would seem to be rooted in life-style factors other than residential energy use - for instance, driving habits (see the following section, **Impacts of the Private Automobile**).

Table 6. Residential energy expenditure by net income in the FRG in 1974

Net income (DM)	Less than 500	500-1000	1000-1500	1500-2000	2000-3000	3000-4000	4000-5000	Greater than 5000	
Expenditure on residential energy	--	61	79	87	95	104	116	150	Average total = 89
Percentage of net income	--	7.9	6.3	5.0	3.9	3.0	2.6	1.9	Average total % = 4.0

Source: Göseke & Bedau (1978)

Because enrichment of all aspects of consumption correlates strongly with income level, some marked differences in the use of absolute residential energy will occur between income classes. (For an example, see Table 6). These differences are even greater if "indirect" household energy use is included in the calculations (see Figure 2). The **burden** of residential energy costs, however, is in inverse proportion to income level - a fact dependent on the large share of total residential energy expenditure for "necessary" heating (e.g., Coe 1980; Uusitalo 1980c).

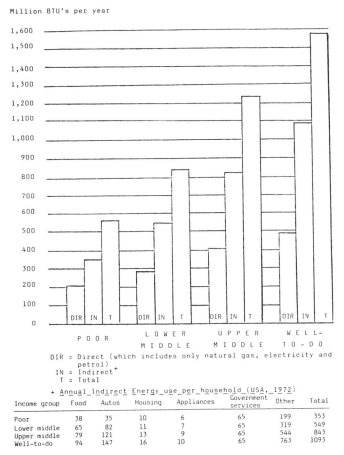

Figure 2. <u>Direct and indirect household energy use
by income group (petrol included)</u>

Million BTU's per year

DIR = Direct (which includes only natural gas, electricity and
      petrol)
IN = Indirect[+]
T = Total

+ <u>Annual Indirect Energy use per household (USA, 1972)</u>

Income group	Food	Autos	Housing	Appliances	Government services	Other	Total
Poor	38	35	10	6	65	199	353
Lower middle	65	82	11	7	65	319	549
Upper middle	79	121	13	9	65	544	843
Well-to-do	94	147	16	10	65	763	1093

The composition of residential energy use varies among countries according to
climate and several structural variables which include, for example,
technological efficiency of appliances, heating and warm-water systems,
insulation norms, saturation and number of new appliances on or coming onto
the market, family pattern and size (Schipper & Ketoff 1980; Schipper 1979).

Behavioural factors affecting residential energy use include the choice of
residential form (e.g., the preference for a single-family or multiple-family

136

dwelling) and the appliance-use intensity. For example, the use of a freezer depends on the food preparation habits of a household (modern versus traditional consumption), the use of dryers on the comfort needs of a household (enriched consumption style) etc. Even in predicting residential heating energy consumption, household behaviour has been stated to be a more important factor than actual, physical characteristics of the house itself (Penz & Yasky 1979).

Impacts of the Private Automobile

The dominance of the private automobile in present-day life-style patterns has environmental consequences in four major areas: energy consumption, land use, air pollution and noise.

Although automobile ownership is a universally adopted value in all countries, there are differences in the per capita petrol consumption which correlate strongly with income level (total private per capita consumption) and hence with the total number of automobiles. A comparison between petrol consumption and income level shows that petrol consumption increases in linear relation to income level (see Figure 3).

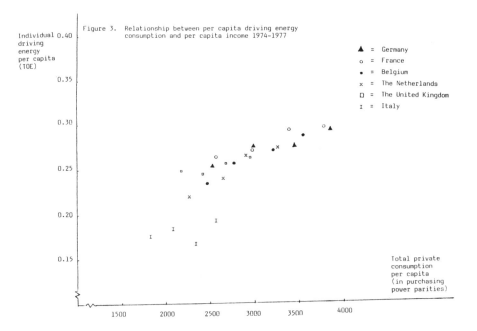

Figure 3. Relationship between per capita driving energy consumption and per capita income 1974-1977

137

While driving distances may offer some explanation for intercountry
differences in petrol consumption, the size of the automobile (and its
engine) - a factor more attributable to life-style **per se** - clearly has an
important effect on this as well. For example, Italians drive small cars and,
as one would naturally expect, have the lowest per car and per capita petrol
consumption. On the other hand, the French have a relatively high percentage
of small and medium-size cars, but still have a higher per car and per capita
petrol consumption than the West Germans, who on average drive bigger cars
(see Figure 4). One possible explanation for this may lie in the difference in
the number of driving family members.

Figure 4. Registered automobiles ordered according to
engine size and driving energy consumption

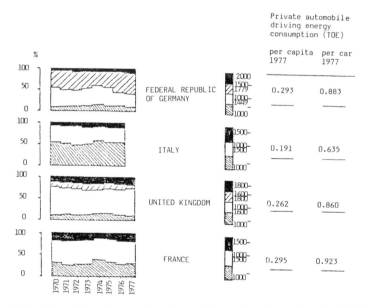

It is difficult to estimate the effect of the price of petrol on individual
driving, because, after an increase in prices in 1974/75, the real price has
decreased (see Table 7). Normally, the income effect overrules the price
effect in all types of energy use within households. Therefore, automobile
prices may also be considered an important factor in conserving energy by
limiting the growth in the number of cars. The burden of petrol prices,
however, is much less regressive than the burden of automobile prices.

Table 7. Energy price evolution of major fuels in the
transport sector in real terms, 1972 = 100

(a) = premium (octane RM 95 and above)
(b) = regular (octane RM 94 and below)

		1973	1974	1975	1976	1977	1978
United Kingdom	(a)	92.6	95.6	139.9	114.5	103.9	92.3
	(b)	94.6	98.8	148.0	128.1	109.2	96.7
The Netherlands	(a)	95.3	103.5	103.2	102.7	99.5	90.2
	(b)	95.6	104.6	104.6	104.0	100.2	91.6
Belgium	(a)	102.5	99.7	109.9	104.0	97.9	81.6
	(b)	102.7	107.5	111.3	106.2	100.1	84.4
Germany	(a)	100.6	112.5	113.6	109.8	106.1	103.7
	(b)	98.6	112.7	115.3	113.3	109.9	107.3
Italy	(a)	90.5	93.6	119.8	108.0	145.2	129.3
	(b)	90.5	94.7	122.1	109.6	148.5	132.1
USA	(a)	(1975=100)		100.0	102.9	101.4	98.9
	(b)	103.4	109.8	111.1	114.6	113.3	109.5

Source: Shonka et al. (eds.), Transportation energy conservation
data book, 1979

Finally, some other environmental impacts of automobile usage deserve
mention. For instance, the share of the population who claimed to be
disturbed by traffic noise grew in West Germany from 35 % in 1960 to 43 % by
1972. Already by the mid-1970s, 72 % of the West German population had been
exposed to a noise level of 55 (Leg. dBA) at its minimum. In 1950, the traffic
system in West Germany required 3.5 % of the land area. By 1972, this figure
had grown to 4.6 % (Zapf 1978). The development in other countries follows
the same trend. With respect to air pollution (again using West Germany as
the example), motor vehicle emissions account for more than one half of total
emissions in a given city in summer and about one third of the total for the
winter months (Geiger 1975).

139

SUMMARY

This article has briefly described three aspects of a qualitative change in consumption patterns which play an important part in influencing environmental externalities of private consumption: (1) "Modernization" of consumption, i.e., the increased use of mass-produced goods and services which, in highly industrialized and urbanized societies, has replaced the home production of commodities; (2) "Enrichment" of consumption, i.e., the increased variety and many-sidedness of the consumption basket due to the higher amount of "free-disposable" income and leisure, and (3) the increased importance of private automobile use in everyday life.

Both modernization and enrichment of consumption have a direct effect on the amount and composition of household waste. Modernization is foremost associated with the increased packaging waste in household refuse (especially paper and glass waste, but also metals and plastics). The littering of highly urbanized surroundings is another symptom.

Enrichment of consumption, in addition to packaging waste, seems to increase the amount of discarded household items (including appliances, textiles and clothing) as well as the amount of food waste. The increased number of electric appliances and the higher standard and larger size of dwellings (and housing models of single-family dwellings), which are typical for an enriched pattern of consumption, are associated with high energy consumption in the household sector.

The heavy emphasis on the private automobile in the transport sector, combined with a higher burden placed on households in the transportation of consumer goods, adds to the growth of energy consumed directly by private households. Enrichment of consumption and automobile ownership together influence mass tourism and its negative aspects. Automobile use alone has also had considerable effects on land use, pollution and noise, especially in high density urban areas.

Some empirical data have been presented here as examples of the above mentioned tendencies. However, the lack of systematically collected data concerning the environmental effects of private consumption is by far the greatest obstacle to research in this field.

140

REFERENCES

A time to choose. (1974). America's Energy Future. Energy policy project of the Ford Foundation. Cambridge, Mass.: Ballinger Publishing Company.

Bergman, L., Clemens, C., & Hoelzl, A. (1979). An input-output analysis of intercountry differences in per capita energy consumption. In: R. Fazzolare & C. Smith (eds.), Changing energy use futures. Los Angeles: Pergamon Press. Pp. 67 - 74

Bergman, L., Clemens, C., & Hoelzl, A. (1980). An input-output approach to the analysis of intercountry differences in per capita energy consumption. Working paper 80-3. The International Institute for Applied Systems Analysis, Laxenburg, Austria.

Coe, R. (1980). A comparison of utility payments and burdens between 1971 and 1977. In: Five thousand American families - Patterns of economic progress, Vol. VIII. Pp. 339 - 386

Geiger, B. (1975). Die Auswirkungen des einbaren Energieansatzes auf das Stadtklima. Gesundheits-Ingenieur, 96 (6), pp. 156 - 160

Giplin, S. (1980). L'utilisation efficace de l'énergie dans les automobiles. BEUC: Study Days of the European Consumer Organizations on the Energy Problem, Paris

Goddard, H. (1976). Managing solid wastes. Economics, technology and institutions. Praeger.

Hill, D. (1980). The relative burden of higher gasoline prices. In: Five thousand American families - Patterns of economic progress, Vol. VIII. Pp. 387 - 413

Hirst, E. (1979). Understanding residential/commercial energy conservation: The need for data. Oak Ridge National Laboratory, September 1979

Jahresgutachten 1979/80 des Sachverständigenrates zur Begutachtung der gesamtwirtschaftlichen Entwicklung. (1979). Wiesbaden

Langer, H., & Stief, K. (1978). Menge und Zusammensetzung von Abfällen. Beihefte zu Mull und Abfall 14. Berlin: Erich Schmidt Verlag

Materialen zum Abfallwirtschaftsprogramm 75 Bundesregierung. Glasabfälle. (1979). Umweltbundesamt.

OECD. Economic Surveys 1970 - 1979

OECD. Energy Balances

OECD. (1978). Beverage containers - refuse or recycling. Paris

Penz, A., & Yasky, Y. (1979). Uncertainties in predicting energy consumption in houses. Energy Systems and Policy, 3 (3), pp. 243 - 269

Pindyck, R. (1979). International comparisons of the residential demand for energy. European Economic Review, 13, pp. 1 - 24

Resource recovery and waste reduction. Fourth report to Congress. U.S. Environmental Protection Agency 1977

Schipper, L. (1979). International analysis of residential energy use and conservation. LBL-9383. Lawrence Berkeley Laboratory, University of California

Schipper, L., & Ketoff, A. (1980). International residential energy and use data: Analysis of historical and present-day structure and dynamics. Proceedings of the Consumer Behavior and Energy Conferences, Alberta, Canada, 1980

Schönfeld, A. (1978). Umwelt und Verpackung aus der Sicht der Abfallwirtschaft. **Mitteilungsdienst der VZ/NTW 1 - 2.**

Shonka, D. et al. (1979). Transportation energy conservation data book. Edition 3. Oak Ridge National Laboratory.

Social indicators for the European Community 1960 - 1975. (1977). EUROSTAT: Statistical Office of the European Communities. Luxembourg-Kirchberg

Social indicators 1976 (–) Selected data on social conditions and trends in the United States. (1977). U.S. Department of Commerce

Statistische Jahrbucher 1970 - 1980. Bundesrepublik Deutschland

Tatsachen und Zahlen aus der Kraftverkaehrswirtschaft. Verband der deutschen Automobilindustrie (VDA)

Uusitalo, L. (1979a). Consumption style and way of life - An empirical identification and explanation of consumption style dimensions. **Acta Academiae Oeconomicae Helsingiensis,** Series A:27. Helsinki

Uusitalo, L. (1979c). The ecological relevance of consumption style. **IIUG/79 - 27. Preprints of the International Institute for Environment and Society, Science Center Berlin**

Uusitalo, L. (1980a). Differentiation of the way of life by technological development, social system and sex - Some tentative findings based on secondary time-use data. **Discussion paper 80-17, The International Institute for Environment and Society,** Science Center Berlin

Uusitalo, L. (1980b). Development of household energy consumption and some assumptions of its social background. **Discussion paper 81-1, The International Institute for Environment and Society,** Science Center Berlin

Uusitalo, L. (1980c). Composition of household energy consumption. **Discussion paper 81-2, The International Institute for Environment and Society,** Science Center Berlin

VDA (1975 - 79). Tatsachen und Zahlen aus der Kraftverkehrswirtschaft. Verband der deutschen Automobilindustrie.

Vogel, G. (1978). Der Beitrag des Recyclings zur Stabilisierung des techno-sozio-ekonomischen Systems. **Schriftenreihe des Instituts Technologie und Warenwirtschaft, 1**

Zapf, W. (ed.) (1978). Lebensbedingungen in der Bundesrepublik. Sozialer Wandel und Wohlfahrtsentwicklung.